NIGEL
MANSELL

THE COMPLETE
PICTORIAL RECORD

NIGEL
MANSELL

THE COMPLETE PICTORIAL RECORD

KEITH SUTTON

Foreword by

Murray Walker

DEDICATION

To Tracey, who has shared my ambitions and dreams for ten years. She married me this year,
allowing me to return the love and patience which she has shown to me for so long.

ACKNOWLEDGEMENTS

I must first thank Nigel Mansell himself for having provided me with so many photographic opportunities throughout his long and distinguished career. I have photographed the many highs and lows. I was in Adelaide in 1986, at the end of the Brabham Straight, when that rear tyre let go so terrifyingly, and could only imagine what he must have been feeling as a well deserved world championship evaporated in a series of wild slides. But I relish in contrast the memory of that wonderful wheel-to-wheel battle with Ayrton Senna on the run down to the first corner at Barcelona in 1992. Nigel, unforgettably, came off best from the encounter; and when at last he clinched the championship that year in Hungary, I was there to capture the emotion of the triumph that he shared, so typically, with his wife Rosanne.

My thanks go to all those who have helped me in my professional life, first among them my parents Maurice and Dawn, who have generously aided and encouraged me. My wife Tracey has given me priceless support. I am also grateful to my brothers Mark and Paul, both photographers, who have helped build Sutton Photographic into the success it is today, alongside my colleagues at work: Kate Sullivan, Gavin Lawrence, Tim Foster, Neil Hepworth and Alex Gardiner.

Special thanks to the loyal friends from our schooldays who have helped through the years in many different ways – Gordon Henshaw, David McIntosh, Philip Stephenson and Simon Woodhams – and in Manchester, Martin Owen, Chris Gardner and Graham Wood. John Brooks, a fine photographer and wise adviser, has been invaluable; as has my bank manager, Howard Ames.

Thanks are due to the photographers who assisted in the preparation of this book: Daniele Amaduzzi, Jeff Bloxham, Roger Calvert, Ercole Colombo, Chris Davies, Martyn Elford, Nigel Kinrade, Carlos Matos, Tim Rempe, Steven Tee, John Townsend. Best wishes to all my friends in Japan, especially Mr Yoshio Asama and the staff at Sony Magazines, and thanks to my agent Massa Okikura for all his hard work.

My gratitude goes also to all the motorsport photographers around the world who supply such excellent material to Sutton Photographic. To all of the drivers, team managers, mechanics and journalists who have contributed to this book I offer my thanks. I value their friendship in the hope that I will be able share it in the years to come.

Keith Sutton

First published in Great Britain in 1995 by Osprey,
an imprint of Reed Consumer Books
Limited, Michelin House, 81 Fulham Road,
London SW3 6RB and Auckland,
Melbourne, Singapore and Toronto

Photographs © Sutton photographic 1995

ISBN 185532 591 8

Managing Editor Shaun Barrington
Editor Dennis Baldry
Art Director Mike Moule
Page design Paul Kime

Printed and bound by Jarrold, Norwich

Half title page: Last outing with the prancing horse and second place for Nigel Mansell at the end of the 1990 season, Adelaide

Title page: Looking extraordinarily relaxed at the first test of the Newman-Haas Lola in January 1993, Phoenix

Opposite: In exalted company, with Ayrton Senna at Estoril, Portugal, September 1990 and (below) another immortal, the great Fangio, Australia in the same year. Philippe Allio on the left, Riccardo Patrese, right

Overleaf: The People's Champion, (above), Silverstone, July 1992. Are you sitting comfortably? Murray Walker asks some probing questions (below) about the MP4/10, Imola 1995

FOREWORD

Whenever I go to Australia I can be sure that someone will come up to me and say 'and how's the President of the Nigel Mansell Fan Club?' It's a bit of a trade mark I've got Down Under and, I hope, everywhere else, for I've never made any secret of my respect and admiration for Nigel, whose career I have followed and enthusiastically talked about since his early Formula Ford days.

And what a career! Having bought this book you won't need telling about his racing life, which Keith Sutton and Mike Doodson have recorded so impressively and comprehensively. But what was the Mansell magic that created such worldwide hero worship? In my view it was a unique blend of race-winning ability, showmanship, courage and an affinity with the people who ultimately paid his considerable wages – the public. The modern Grand Prix driver is a remote and unattainable figure to most of his followers. If they're lucky and have made the considerable investment in the right tickets, they can see but certainly cannot touch, let alone talk to, their idols. But Mansell always made himself as available as possible, even to the extent of living in a motor home at Silverstone during the British Grand Prix and spending many hours signing autographs and chatting with his fans. Sophisticated and devious he most definitely is not. That he is a steak and chips, Union Jack, man of the people is exemplified by the fact that in his mega-earning days it was to the Isle of Man that he went, legitimately to avoid tax, rather than to Monaco (the traditional Formula 1 millionaire's haven), whilst in his new life he has settled near Exeter to develop new endeavours around his beloved golf.

But, more than anything else in my view, his racing appeal was down to total commitment, the fact that he drove the wheels off anything he was in and that he had enough courage for ten men. Nigel took a race by the throat and never let go. And they didn't call him 'Il Leone' in Italy for nothing. When Mansell was at the wheel he gave it ten-tenths and where he was things seemed to happen in a way they seldom did with his blander rivals. It was Nigel who collapsed in the searing heat of Dallas 1984 as he tried to push his broken Lotus to the line. A furious Nigel who had the physical confrontation with Ayrton Senna at Spa in 1987. Nigel who executed those sensational passing moves on Senna and Gerhard Berger in Hungary and Mexico. Nigel who had his wheel come off in the pitlane in Portugal, a wheel nut come off in Hungary and who won his first race for Ferrari in Brazil when everyone was convinced he would be lucky to last ten laps. And Nigel who always seemed to be at odds with somebody about something.

At the wheel he captivates. Out of the cockpit he is not always the easiest man in the world to get on with. In life few people get to the top by being relaxed, easy going and undemanding and he certainly didn't. He's a perfectionist, he is ultra-sensitive, takes offence easily and isn't slow to complain when he does. But we've all got drawbacks and although I'm no psychologist I've always thought that Nigel's make up results in him being the sort of driver that he is. Tough on those around him but even tougher on himself. Demanding, dogged, determined, ultra-aggressive and incredibly quick. If proof were needed – which it certainly isn't – think of the countless battles he had with that other unyielding superstar Ayrton Senna. In particular Spain in 1986, when he caught Ayrton after a tyre stop only eight laps from the end of the race to be beaten by a mere 1/100th of a second, and Monaco 1992 where his recovery drive after a late stop and his efforts to get past Senna made for some of the most exciting racing I have ever seen.

And let's not forget his incredible year in America. He went there amidst predictions that he was biting off more than he could chew, instantly conquered the highly-specialised ovals, blew his much-vaunted rivals away and unprecedentedly won the championship in the first year. Watching him very nearly win the fabled Indianapolis 500 at his first attempt was one of the most most rivetting experiences of my life.

But now I'm wandering down memory lane in a situation where it is all here in your hands, for you to reminisce over and enjoy. Before you do I'd just like to pay tribute both to Nigel and his strong-minded and charming wife Rosanne, without whom I'm sure he would not have achieved what he has, as real friends who have been helpful, patient and understanding of my many demands on them over the years and to say that I hope he does as well at his second career – making a possibly fatal assumption! – as he has at his first. Knowing him I have no doubt that he will.

Murray Walker
8th August 1995

INTRODUCTION

As a photographer, my memories of the great moments in motorsport are all visual. Thanks either to good judgement or, occasionally, sheer luck, I have seen many of the sport's most memorable images through the viewfinder of my own camera. Some of the excitement of the photographer's work is the anticipation of seeing the processed film on the light box. Even after 15 years, there is still the thrill of seeing one of my own photographs published.

For me, Grand Prix racing will always be a spellbinding sport, packed with the tension that comes when the power of the cars and the talents of their drivers are matched on the track.

With Nigel Mansell there were plenty of those tense moments. Even if his car was even only half competitive, Nigel was almost unstoppable. There were times when I was entirely content to be behind a camera rather than a driver, however well paid, in a car that was about to be gobbled up by him. My sympathy always went to those in their hot cockpits trying to check the mirrors to be ready when the man in the stripey helmet steamrollered his way through.

These days the TV coverage of Grands Prix is so good that the viewer can take it for granted that he or she is not going to be deprived of the most significant and spectacular incidents. Viewers also know that they will be replayed in slow motion and from several different angles.

Alone on the circuit, limited to a small section of the track, the photographer can only hope that some of the action will happen on his 'patch'. With Nigel I was fortunate to be right there at two of the decisive moments in his career.

At Adelaide in 1986 I was one of a handful of photographers stationed at the end of Brabham Straight when his rear tyre let go, costing him the 1986 championship. At Barcelona in 1991 I saw him challenge Senna's McLaren-Honda in that extended episode of wheel-to-wheel bravado which signalled that Williams, Renault and Nigel Mansell were in the ascendant. And in Hungary in 1992 I shared the joy that followed his clinching of the title with one of the few second places that made him completely happy.

There were many other memorable Mansell moments. I never imagined, for example, that I would see a crowd as devoted to its hero as the fans who had packed themselves into Sao Paulo's Interlagos stadium to see Ayrton Senna win the Brazilian GP at his eighth attempt in 1991. Just over a year later, though, I was almost literally carried away as thousands of exultant British fans swept over the fences and barriers at Silverstone to greet Nigel's historic victory in the British GP.

Nigel's appeal to the public has been endlessly discussed and analysed. I do not intend to add to the debate except to recall that he was, and is, a man who does not hide his emotions. Delight, triumph, disappointment and pain regularly showed up on that moustached face and in my pictures.

I believe that race fans loved him because they could see something of themselves in him. He wasn't a rich man's son and when he went karting with his father it was in much the same spirit as the thousands of small boys who go fishing with their dads at the weekend. He had worked in a factory, he had scraped together his savings and he had blown the lot on a Formula 3 drive. This was hard-earned wages that he had spent, not the advertising budget of some big company. It was something with which anyone who has earned a wage packet can identify.

They loved him in other countries, too. Inevitably Italy took to him when he joined Ferrari in 1989, and the love affair had a brilliant start when he won that extraordinary first race with the Scuderia in Brazil. But the true mark of the tifosi's respect for Nigel didn't come until after the Ferrari passions had cooled and he returned to Williams. Even then, the banners continued to wave as vigorously as ever for the man they dubbed 'Il Leone' – the Lion.

This book is a tribute to Nigel. Unusually, it consists mostly of photographs. It happens that the start of my career in racing photography in 1977 coincided with Nigel's beginnings in Formula Ford. In 1980, shortly before Nigel made his first F1 appearance with Lotus in Austria, I had taken the plunge and turned professional.

If I followed him a little more closely then than some of the other drivers, it was probably because we were both new boys, both British, and I wanted success for him just as much as I did for myself. I cannot claim a close friendship with him, although circumstances frequently threw us together.

I will always be grateful to him for the support he showed for racing photographers and for FOPA, our own professional body, when he agreed to play for us in a football 'friendly'. He put as

Nigel with the two men whose faith ultimately made him world champion: Frank Williams (left), owner of the team he first joined in 1985; and Peter Collins, the Australian who spotted his ability in 1979 and later served as team manager both at Lotus and Williams

much energy into that game as he would have used on a qualifying lap. As on the track, so on the soccer pitch: he was like an express train. Fortunately, my camera was ready for the occasions when he came off the rails – and when he didn't.

At the time of writing, Nigel Mansell's career as a racing driver was in some doubt as far as the media was concerned. At the age of 42, they say, he should be satisfied with his world championship and his IndyCar title, not to mention his 31 Grand Prix victories and all the other records. Nigel himself has left no doubt at all about his willingness to return. He insists that he is ready to answer the call whenever, and from wherever, it may come.

Meanwhile, we are left with our memories. For me, many of them are permanently recorded on film. As you share them on the pages that follow, I hope that you will be reminded of the achievements of this determined, fearless and obstinate sportsman. There will surely never be anyone quite like him again.

Keith Sutton
Northamptonshire, England
3rd August, 1995

Off duty – insofar as a man as famous as Nigel Mansell can ever be off duty. At the Renault UK 90th anniversary (top left), driving a 1902 Renault 14 CU alongside the Williams FW14. Relaxing on the Isle of Man (top right) and before the 1992 British GP at the Buckingham Golf Club (centre left). Family outing at Monaco, 1992 (centre right). Mansell was actually given a horse in Hungary in 1991!

THE FAMILY MANSELL 1977-79

Nigel and Rosanne Mansell celebrated their 20th wedding anniversary in April 1975. The strength of their marriage and the happiness which they share in their three children represents something priceless to them both. Nigel has always credited Rosanne with supporting his ambitions, however crazy they may have seemed.

Eric and Joyce Mansell's second son was born (on 8 August 1953) above the cafe which they were running in Upton-on-Severn in Worcestershire. When they moved closer to Birmingham, Eric took up karting, and Nigel would go to the races with him. He had already learned to drive on farmland, and when he got his own kart he was quick. He always insisted that he inherited his speed from Joyce, who enjoyed driving the family car as fast as possible!

The youngster had his first kart race at the age of 10. One year later he was wearing the green helmet of a member of the England kart team. He was regularly accompanied abroad by his two sisters. He often needed them to comfort him in hospital, because his karts were secondhand and frequently broke important components like the steering.

At school he had to catch up the time that he took off to go karting. Although he has never claimed to have been a good student, he passed two O-levels and was able to find a good job at Lucas Aerospace, working for a while alongside his father. His training there, together with attendance at various Technical Colleges, led to an HND. It gave him a grounding in engineering and electronics that would later come in useful.

The newlyweds bought a two-bedroomed house in Birmingham and Rosanne stayed at work. Although Nigel was determined to continue racing, at 21 karting had lost its appeal. Trying a rented Formula Ford at the racing school at Mallory Park in 1976 convinced him that he had a future as a single-seater driver.

Without hesitating, Rosanne agreed that they should spend the £2,000 that would be required to set Nigel up with a Formula Ford and trailer. Driving this (well) used Hawke he won his first 'clubbie' at Mallory Park, and there were sufficient other good results to support the belief which Rosanne shared in his ability. Early in 1977, he decided to give up his job at Lucas to concentrate on racing.

In June he suffered the first of the three or four serious accidents which threatened to put an end to the career which he had planned for himself. Driving in the wet during practice for an FF race at Brands Hatch, he was forced off the dry line by a slower competitor. Crashing backwards into a barrier, he sustained two breaks to the neck. Disregarding warnings from the doctors that he might have to remain flat on his back for several months, a few days later he discharged himself from the hospital. Using a neck brace, within a few weeks he was racing and winning again. Despite the layoff, he even managed to win the Brush Fusegear Championship.

Nigel felt that his record of 33 victories from 42 heats and races in Formula Ford justified a move into Formula 3. He decided, once again with Rosanne's support, to invest in a factory drive with the March team. There were promises of help and hints of sponsorship, but first he had to raise some cash. He did so by selling the flat which he had bought a couple of years earlier, raising £6,000 towards the £8,000 that March required from him.

The money bought five races with a car that was a long way from being competitive. The promised backup never materialised and there were no results worth mentioning. Nigel's only consolation that year was a handful of saloon cars races against established drivers in the BMW County Championship. Among those taking note had been team boss David Price, who offered Nigel a paid drive for 1979 in one of the March F3 cars that he was running for Unipart.

With a quirky engine derived from that installed in the Triumph Dolomite Sprint saloon, the Unipart March was rarely competitive. However, Nigel at last scored an F3 win, at Silverstone in the race which supported that year's International Trophy race. He also raced the car at Monaco, where the Unipart cars had become something of a joke. Nigel loved racing on the famous circuit and finished 11th.

Two months later, on the day before the British GP at Silverstone, he met Lotus chief Colin Chapman. It was Australian-born Peter Collins, Lotus's manager, who introduced the team owner and the 25-year-old driver. Chapman gave Mansell some encouragement and a few days later Collins – who had already spotted something special in Nigel's style – offered him a part-time job as a parts-chaser. Nigel gratefully accepted both.

That brief conversation with Chapman would prove to have been the single most important move that Nigel would make towards GP glory.

Leo proudly escorts his father to work: Silverstone, 1991

A flight (top) in a British Aerospace Hawk of the RAF's Red Arrows, a cuddle with daughter Chloe. Altogether at Monaco (below) in 1992: Rosanne, Chloe, Leo and Greg

Two early Formula Ford races in 1976 at Mallory Park with the Hawke DL11 that he picked up for less than £2,000

At Thruxton (top) with the unreliable but occasionally quick "works" Javelin in 1977 and (below) leading at Oulton Park with a Crossle

More Formula Ford in 1977 aboard a factory Crosslé 32F, with the sponsor's name writ large …

Early F3 days (top) at Silverstone with a borrowed Lola T570 in 1977; and the satisfaction of winning the Brush Fusegear FF title only weeks after discharging himself from hospital following neck injuries

The F3 gamble in 1977 (top) with a one-off Puma at Silverstone; and (below) one of the five races with March which cost Nigel and Rosanne their life savings

A rare picture (top) of the ICI-sponsored Chevron F2 which Nigel had to hand over to renta-driver Elio de Angelis at Donington Park in 1978. Struggling (below) to keep the Unipart March-Triumph ahead of the pack

The first (and only) F3 victory with Unipart, on International Trophy day at Silverstone, 25 March 1979

Upside down at Foster's Corner, Oulton Park, after the F3 incident with Andrea de Cesaris which gave Nigel another pain in the neck

The Mansell partnership paid off in 1981, the first full year of F1 with Lotus

Sharing a trade secret with Brazilian Roberto Moreno, briefly Lotus's test driver in 1982

Tarmac terrors meet the giants of the gravel at the televised Donington Park Rallysprint in 1981: with McLaren rival John Watson (top) and rally star Tony Pond; and (below) leading 1980 world champion Alan Jones

Back to Donington for the 1982 Rallysprint and Nigel's turn to try a Toyota (top) on the rough. Rallymen fight back (below) in the circuit event

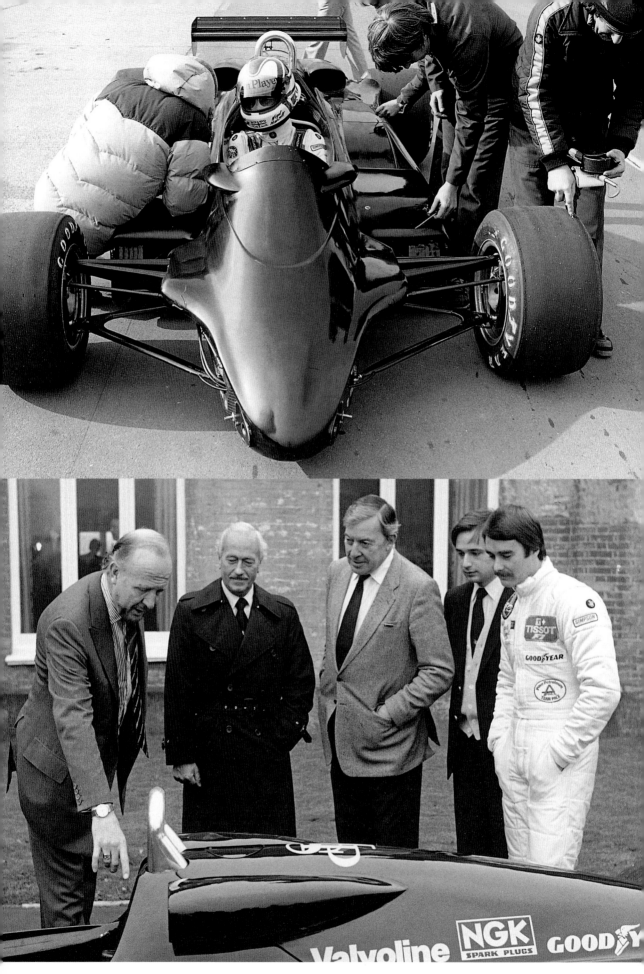

First test in the (still unstickered) Lotus 91 which was rushed into service in mid-season 1982, with executives of returning sponsor John Player (below) flanking Lotus chief Colin Chapman as Nigel watches alongside team mate Elio de Angelis

The law takes an interest (top) at Silverstone in 1982: Nigel himself later became a Special Constable. Some man-handling (below) for the new Lotus 91 at Dijon (France) during the one-off Swiss GP meeting

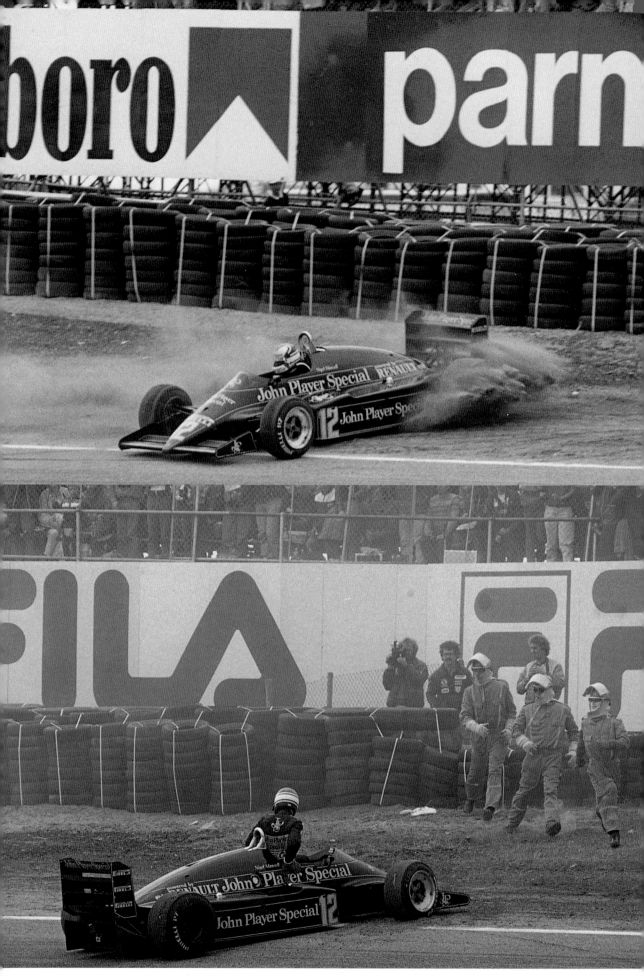

Spinning but safe at Zandvoort after brake problems put an end to his chances in the 1982 Dutch GP. We're far ahead of ourselves in this section of course, but the Lotus team rather suits black and white…

With race winner Nelson Piquet (top), Nigel celebrates a hard-earned 3rd place in the European GP at Brands Hatch. At ease in Monaco (below), a circuit which he loved but where victories were snatched from his grasp on at least three occasions

At last! That great victory with Williams at Brands Hatch in 1985 and Rosanne fights back the tears as she prepares to share the victory lap with Nigel and his team mate Keke Rosberg

Concentrating before the start of the 1985 Portuguese GP at Estoril

An early outing for Nigel in the well-used Hawke FF car (top) which he and Rosanne bought in 1976. Cornering energetically at Donington (below) in 1977 with one of the BMW 323i touring cars which contested the County championships

Close dicing at Silverstone: in 1977 (top) with a factory Crossle; and (below) in 1979 with the Unipart March, the first car that Nigel was paid to drive

With its heavy and unresponsive 16-valve engine derived from the sporty Triumph Dolomite saloon, the Unipart March scored its only victory (top) at Silverstone

After a full season in 1979 with the Unipart March, Nigel contested a handful of F3 races in 1980 with a fully supported March-Toyota. But his mind was already fixed on his F1 contract with Lotus

Thruxton (top left), March 1980, second outing of the season and fourth place in the Vandervell F3 race. Three months later (top right) and the Malboro F2 Trophy at Silverstone. Then into the big time with Team Essex Lotus a few weeks later at the Dutch GP (centre left). Lotus Team Managers: Peter Collins being put straight by Colin Chapman (bottom left), Buenos Aires, 1981, and Peter Warr (centre right) in glasses, Brazil 1982 – the latter not a Nigel Mansell fan. Monte Carlo, 1981 (bottom right), one of eight retirements during the season

SUCCESS AT LAST 1980-83

At last Nigel had something to justify his dreams. Peter Collins, who would remain a good friend in the coming years, had told him that Lotus would be testing drivers for the F1 team at the end of the year. Chapman had listened to Collins' descriptions of Nigel's driving, and he liked what he heard about the late-braking style which even then was his speciality. Meanwhile, he continued with the Unipart F3 car. At Oulton Park in September 1979, while scrapping for second place, he was pushed off the road in an impossible overtaking manoeuvre by Andrea de Cesaris. After a series of rolls, he finished up underneath the car. With broken vertebrae and and other injuries, the hospital authorities again warned him that racing would be out of the question for weeks, maybe months.

A month later he was still at home recovering when he got the message that the Lotus F1 test was on – and he was invited. Peter Collins concealed the information from Chapman that Nigel was so full of painkilling tablets that he was almost rattling. Nigel behaved well: he adapted quickly to F1 power and only spun once. The drive for 1980 went to one of the other four drivers, Elio de Angelis. Nigel, though, was eventually offered a position as Lotus's test driver.

For the 1980 season Nigel had lined up a handful of F3 outings and four races with the Ralt-Honda factory team. Although none produced a win, Nigel didn't care too much. Far more important to him was the link with Lotus. He was soon being called to stand in at short notice for de Angelis or Mario Andretti in test sessions. Whether it was the moustaches or their shared pride in being British, there was no denying that he and Chapman had hit it off.

Nigel rewarded Chapman's faith with some impressive testing times. In August, Chapman repaid the compliment by allowing Nigel to race the T-car in the Austrian GP. It gave trouble in qualifying and he only just squeaked into the field at the wheel of Elio's car, taking 26th place on the 26-car grid.

It was not a great GP debut. Even before the start he was in pain from fuel that had been spilled into his cockpit. Sluicing it with water was only a temporary measure and before the race was a few laps old he was in appalling pain from petrol burns on his backside and legs. He was in 13th place when the engine mercifully blew up with 13 laps to go. He needed medical attention when he returned to England.

Promised two more GPs with Lotus in 1980, he had no luck. At Zandvoort his brakes failed and at Imola he failed to qualify. But he had done enough to persuade Chapman that he was the right man to take over from Andretti when the American signed for Alfa Romeo.

Nigel would spend five full years at Lotus. He scored his first points when he came home third at Zolder, Belgium, in the fifth GP of the season – ahead of his team mate de Angelis. But he was destined to finish only twice more in the points that year. Colin Chapman had been working on a complex car with a twin-chassis arrangement designed to stretch the rules. After several confrontations with officials in different countries, it was vetoed. Lotus had wasted a lot of effort.

Even though the new Lotus 87 was a difficult car to set up, the 1982 season produced a memorable victory. De Angelis beat Keke Rosberg's Williams in the closest finish that anyone could remember. Nigel picked up only seven points. There was the compensation of the birth in August of Chloe, although December brought the death of Colin Chapman. The new management would be much less sympathetic towards Nigel.

In 1983 Lotus was still changing from Ford V8 to Renault V6 turbo power. As second driver, Nigel had to make do with the old car and engine. Nevertheless, in September he finished third behind Nelson Piquet and Alain Prost with a huge British crowd to support him in the European GP at Brands Hatch. That result, and the intervention of Players (the team's principal sponsor), saved his place at Lotus for 1984.

That season, Nigel's last at Lotus, should have been memorable. It was – for all the wrong reasons. At Monaco there was the famous incident when he spun off in the rain on a white stripe painted in the road. It didn't help that he had been leading. Then there was Dallas, where he collapsed in the heat while trying (illegally) to push his crippled car over the line. And the $6,000 fine he had to pay at Detroit when accused of triggering an accident at the start.

At the Dutch GP, Lotus manager Peter Warr – the man with whom Nigel had been in conflict for two years – happily announced that a newcomer named Ayrton Senna would be taking the Lotus drive alongside de Angelis for 1984. At the same race meeting, Nigel had a meeting with Frank Williams which persuaded the team owner to sign him: against his better judgment?

With more help from sponsors, there was an opportunity in 1980 to race a factory Ralt-Honda in Formula 2

After leading this European championship F2 race at Hockenheim almost to the finish, Nigel dropped to 2nd place behind Teo Fabi (with champagne) due to fuel pressure trouble

Close fighting at Zolder in a Belgian round of the European F2 championship

Keeping a close eye on his Lotus during the weekend of the Austrian GP at the Osterreichring in August 1980, Nigel's very first race in a world championship event

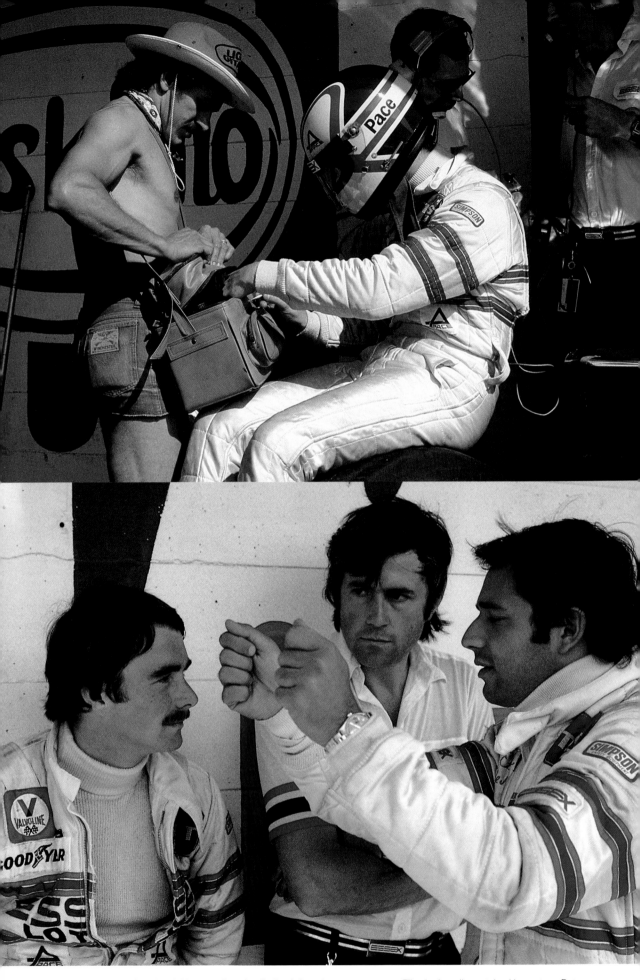

Pit scenes in Austria: picking up a few tips (below) from Lotus team mate Elio de Angelis, watched by a stern Peter Wright (team engineer)

The Lotus 79X which Nigel drove in Austria (top) and Holland was hardly state of the art: those were to be his only two starts with the Ford-powered car

Full time F1 driver at last: (top) in South Africa and (below) larking with Rosanne and TV man Andrew Marriott

Preparing to qualify at Kyalami for the "rogue" South African GP of 1981. There were no points, but Nigel was especially impressive during a rain storm that fell during the race

Buenos Aires, 1981: after Lotus chief Colin Chapman had argued in vain to have the "twin chassis" Lotus 88 accepted, Nigel raced the car converted to conventional type 81 specification. Its Ford engine blew after three laps

Pit scene in Buenos Aires (top) with team manager Peter Collins (right), a staunch supporter and friend to Nigel. First podium (below), in Belgium 1981, where Nigel finished 3rd behind Reutemann and Laffite

Long Beach, 1981: Nigel stays in touch with race engineer Nigel Stroud. Having qualified 7th, he failed to finish after an accident

Mean streets of Long Beach, 1981, where Nigel crashed, possibly as a result of damage sustained during the warm-up session on race morning

Always at his best through the streets of Monaco, Nigel chases Gilles Villeneuve's Ferrari for 2nd place. After Nigel's suspension failed and Piquet crashed, Villeneuve went through to win

Keeping out of the sun at Jarama, 1981, where Nigel picked up one point for 6th place in the Spanish GP

Waiting in Spain: Nigel prepares for the start at Jarama in 1981

The learning process with Lotus: on the way to 7th place in the French GP at Dijon (top); and a glance for Rosanne at the Osterreichring, where his race ended with an engine failure

Putting a brave face on things at Monza in 1981, where the handling of his Lotus was so worrying that he was forced to withdraw

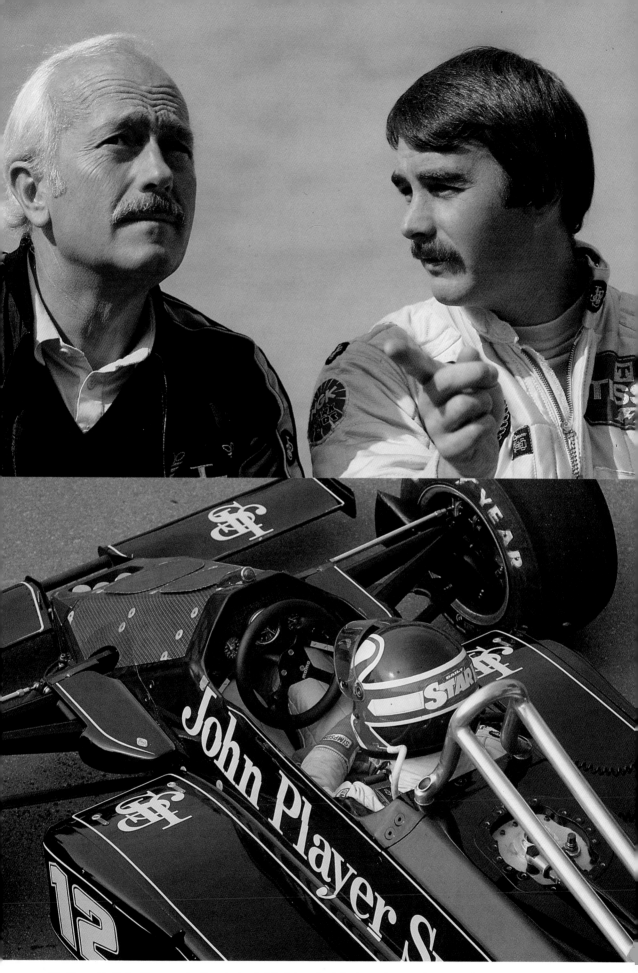

Chatting with Colin Chapman in Canada (top): Nigel described the Lotus boss as "a second father."
Nigel prepares for the race (below), which ended in a misunderstanding with Alain Prost in the rain

Las Vegas 1981 and a finish at last for Nigel, who brought the Lotus through the desert heat to finish 4th

At Silverstone (top) with the Lotus in "twin chassis" specification before the inquisitive FIA officials ruled it illegal. A sponsor's representative gets a look at Nigel's office before the 1982 Brazilian GP

On the way to 4th place in the Long Beach GP of 1982

Having met a couple of patrolman while speeding to a sponsors' function at Long Beach in 1982, Nigel made friends with the cops – who then taught him to shoot straight

The street fighter at Monaco in 1982

Coming round the swimming pool at Monaco on the way to 4th place in the 1982 Grand Prix

Some torrid moments in the pits during 1982, including a public confrontation with fellow-Brit Brian Henton after qualifying at Dijon

Still with the Ford engine (top) in Brazil, the 1983 season started out as a tough period while waiting for the Renault turbo. At Ricard (below) the local scenery passes by unnoticed …

While team mate de Angelis had Renault power from the start of the 1983 season, Nigel had to struggle along with the cumbersome Lotus 92 and Ford V8 power. Here in Brazil he finished 12th

Making friends in 1983: at Imola with the Giacobazzi hostesses; at Silverstone with Jacques Laffite; in Austria with team mate Elio de Angelis; and at Brands Hatch with Nelson Piquet and the Moet

Taking a squint (top) at the machinery in Brazil with manager Peter Warr and mechanic Paul Simpson. Bad luck again in Belgium (below), where he stopped with clutch failure

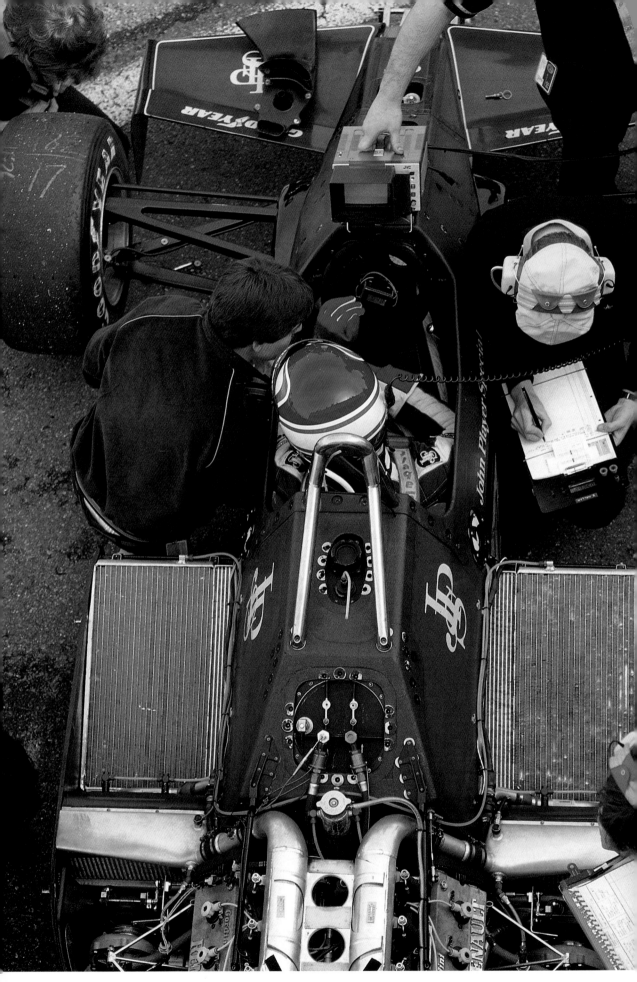

Preparing to qualify at Dijon before the 1984 French GP, in which he finished for the first time that season – and took 3rd place

Monaco 1984, the heartbreak GP in which Nigel qualified 2nd only to spin off the wet track while leading quite comfortably

Moments before the accident at Monaco which took Nigel out of the race after he had taken the lead from Alain Prost and led for five laps. Nigel believed that had touched a white line and broken traction for one vital instant

Montreal 1984: the Canadian race was frequently cruel to Nigel, who at least managed to pick up one point this time around

Memories of 1984 (top), including footballing in Canada with the gentlemen of the press, and an inflated cowboy in Dallas. A few words in the Brands Hatch pit lane (below) with mechanic Paul Simpson

Second visit of the 1984 season to the podium at Zandvoort, where Nigel holds tight to his trophy

Portugal 1984, where Nigel played what would have been a crucial role in the world championship duel between McLaren drivers Lauda and Prost – until his brakes overheated and failed

Qualifying at Monaco in 1984 (top left), Nigel leads Lauda's McLaren – race day would be wet. First Williams test (centre left) at the Donington RallySprint in November 1984. Sport and show business chums: at the Dallas GP, (where else?), soap star Patrick "Bobby Ewing" Duffy (top right) and champion golfer and close friend Greg Norman, Adelaide 1986 (bottom left). Wheel to wheel at Monaco 1985 (centre right) with Ayrton Senna's Lotus; and planning strategy (bottom right) with Frank Williams before the 1987 Monaco GP

WILLIAMS AND VICTORY 1985-87

It was no secret that Keke Rosberg, who had already been with Williams for two years and had won the world championship there in 1982, was not happy about the prospect of being teamed with Nigel. He had even threatened to leave Williams if the deal went through. When it did, Nigel was left in no doubt that he was the number two driver on the team.

But Nigel was to be a useful asset for Keke in the struggle to persuade Honda to improve the power, and particularly the driveability, of the V6 turbo engine. Nigel perhaps lacked the subtlety of a great diplomat, but he had worked with the Honda technicians in 1980 when he raced the factory Ralt-Honda in four F2 races. Together, they started to see some real progress.

This was vital to Nigel. Although 1985 was his fifth season in grand prix racing, he was not yet living up to the promise which had so impressed Colin Chapman and others. He had only made three appearances on the podium, all

for third place, and he badly needed to win.

The breakthrough came very quickly and suddenly, towards the end of the season, in Belgium. Until then he had scored some modest placings but had failed to shine except – as usual – on street circuits like Monaco and Detroit. In qualifying for the Belgian race, he showed a new approach. BBC commentator and former F1 world champion James Hunt – previously no fan of Nigel's – spotted it and was so convinced that the Mansell attitude had changed that he told viewers, on air, that he had placed an each-way bet on Nigel. When Nigel finished second behind Ayrton Senna, Hunt could not have been happier.

The next race, the European GP at Brands Hatch, was to be the real breakthrough. Rosberg and Piquet helped by hitting each other early in the proceedings, but there was still Ayrton Senna to beat. When Keke came out of the pits after an unscheduled stop to change a cut tyre

The breakthrough: second place behind Ayrton Senna at Spa, September 1985, to be followed by two wins at Brands Hatch and Kyalami

Things hadn't been so easy earlier in the season. Extinguisher in hand, Mansell's drive at Montreal '85 ends on the start/finish straight as marshals tackle the flames from his Canon Williams Honda. He had done enough to finish in 6th place and gain world championship points, but the next three races would not include a finish

on lap nine, Senna and Mansell were coming up behind him. Maybe Keke placed his car to suit Williams' strategy, maybe not. The consequence was that Nigel got through in the lead, which is where he stayed, defeating the man who had taken over his Lotus drive by 20 seconds.

The British crowd was delirious with joy. Later Nigel said how much he had been boosted by their support. But there was also a tearful Rosanne to greet him, and elsewhere in the pit lane Eric Mansell shared the joy. Some of the glory was stolen because fourth place had given Alain Prost his first world championship. But Nigel had only two weeks to wait before he got all the limelight. In the very next race, in South Africa, he won again. How, we all wondered, had he taken 72 races to score his first F1 win?

The successes came at the right moment for Frank Williams, who was about to lose Rosberg to McLaren. Nigel's late rush put him into sixth place in the championship and gave his confidence exactly the boost it needed to cope with the arrival of Rosberg's replacement, who was to be Nelson Piquet.

Nigel would later say that he never had a relationship with Nelson. It started badly and got worse. Part of the reason was that in August 1985 when Nelson was signed, already twice a world champion, it was clear that Nigel — still without a win — would continue to be number two. But there were clashes of personality, too. With his happy family background and something of a straitlaced attitude to Nelson's horseplay, Nigel may have often found his team mate's pranks both cruel and distasteful.

Sadly, Frank Williams himself was destined not to be on the spot to sort out the arguments. In March 1986, as he dashed away after a test at the Ricard circuit in southern France, he ran off the road in his hire car and sustained the spinal injuries that deprived him of the use of his lower limbs. It would be 12 months before Frank could resume his duties, now from a wheelchair.

Williams had a super-competitive car that year. Nigel started to amass victories: in the course of the year he won five GPs. Piquet, with his mind perhaps more concentrated on picking up points, scored four wins. By the time they arrived in Australia for the final race of the season, the two of them were in contention for the championship. So, too, was Alain Prost.

Piquet has always maintained that if the team had maintained its promises to him as the nominated number one, issuing 'hold back' instructions to Nigel that would have guaranteed the title for Williams (and himself), then the championship would have been settled before the Australian GP. Instead, the scene was set for a nightmare – and for the TV images which will haunt Nigel for the rest of his life.

To be sure of the title, Nigel needed third place. Having beaten Piquet and Prost into second and third places on the grid, he felt this was a reasonable hope. After Prost had punctured a tyre, the pattern of the race looked good: Rosberg leading from Piquet, with a contented Nigel in third place. When Rosberg stopped with 19 laps to go, out on the back straight, it looked like a Mansell certainty.

Rosberg believed at first that his engine had failed. He had felt a vibration of such intensity that he just pulled to the side of the road. In fact, one of his rear tyres had delaminated, causing the vibration. Driving his cautious race, Nigel had wanted to stop for tyres at half distance but had been discouraged from doing so because Piquet planned a non-stop run.

One lap after Rosberg stopped, Nigel was coming down the Brabham straight at maximum speed when a rear tyre exploded. Almost everyone else in the world saw it on TV, but I saw it through the telephoto lens of my camera. I was one of only three photographers shooting at the end of the straight, which is the best passing place at Adelaide.

To get into position I had just crossed the nearby circuit bridge. I only just arrived in time to catch the Williams weaving from side to side. As he ran straight ahead into the escape road I had to switch from my 500 mm lens to a camera with a shorter lens on it. As I did so, the car twitched like an animal in its death throes and the rear tyre, with its tread now almost loose, flailed the air.

Prost could not believe his luck. He had won the championship from Nigel by just two points, 72-70, and he performed a little dance of joy on the start-finish line as he stepped from his McLaren.

Nigel's second year alongside Piquet in 1987 had no such climax. Again, he won more races than his team mate (six to Piquet's three), but maybe he was trying too hard to win. After a nasty fright at Imola, where he crashed during first qualifying session due to a tyre failure, Piquet put the emphasis even more on consistency. In addition to his wins he was placed second on seven occasions: Nigel only finished in the top three when he won.

Nevertheless, there was still an outside chance for Nigel when he arrived at Suzuka for the Japanese GP. In qualifying on Friday, that chance evaporated when he seemed to lose control and slid wide in an ess-bend. The Williams rode over a kerb, bounced off a tyre barrier and landed, hard, back on the kerb. Nigel's hopes were gone. The agony on his face as he was rescued showed dramatically and he returned that night to the Isle of Man, where 'spinal concussion' was diagnosed.

"DNS" at Japan and Australia: Nelson Piquet automatically became world champion.

Second time out with Williams, at Estoril in a wet 1985 Portuguese GP. After starting from the pit lane, Nigel finished 5th

Having qualified 2nd at Monaco in 1985, Nigel's race was spoiled by brake problems which afflicted both Williams: he lost 6th place to Laffite's Ligier with two laps left to run

With Williams team-mate Keke Rosberg in Canada 1985 (top): after a shaky start he and the Finn became good friends. Montreal misery once more (below) as a "technical problem" halts the Williams again in qualifying. Nigel got to the finish of the race itself, in 6th place

Having qualified 2nd for the 1985 Detroit GP, Nigel found once again that the brakes of the Williams wilted quickly. He crashed into a wall and suffered a concussion

Silverstone 1985: having gambled on hard compound tyres, Nigel suffered a repeat of a clutch problem which his car had suffered in practice

Abandoned at Monza (top) after an incident in qualifying for the 1985 Italian GP, the Williams-Honda is left with three wheels. Better fortunes at Spa (below) where a sparkling 2nd place was a sign of things to come

The Big Day at last, Brands Hatch in October 1985, and Nigel's long-awaited Grand Prix victory, in the European GP. It had taken 72 races to arrive at this special moment

Two in a row: celebrating at Brands (top) with 2nd placeman (and new world champion) Alain Prost after the 1985 European GP. Two weeks later the Williams pit crew anticipate the repeat performance in South Africa (below) one lap before the chequered flag

More celebrations, this time with team mate Rosberg, at Kyalami after the South Africa GP. Out come the Union flags (below), a ritual which Nigel would see many times in the next ten years

Nelson Piquet

Nigel Mansell

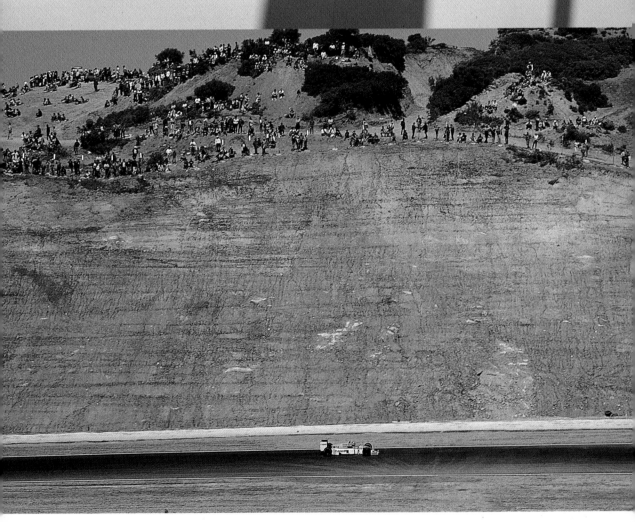

Jerez, Spain, in 1986 and someone's got those names in the wrong order: the bleak Spanish circuit didn't attract a big crowd in its first year

Swapping hats with the Tio Pepe hostesses before the 1986 Spanish GP in the heart of sherry-growing country was a happier occasion than the Monaco GP (below), where the Honda engine was wrongly geared and Nigel had to be content with 4th place

A majestic victory at Spa in the 1986 Belgian GP was tempered by the loss, one week earlier, of Elio de Angelis in an accident at Ricard while testing his Brabham. As team mates at Lotus, Nigel and Elio had formed a strong friendship

Montreal 1986 and Nigel's only victory in the Canadian GP. The Williams-Honda was in a class of its own and the victory – his fourth in F1 – made him a strong contender for the world title

Celebrating his third success of the 1986 season, Nigel gets used to be being only one point behind Alain Prost in the championship

Pondering the task of beating his own team mate in the 1986 British GP, Nigel got everything right on the day (below) and fought off Piquet to win narrowly

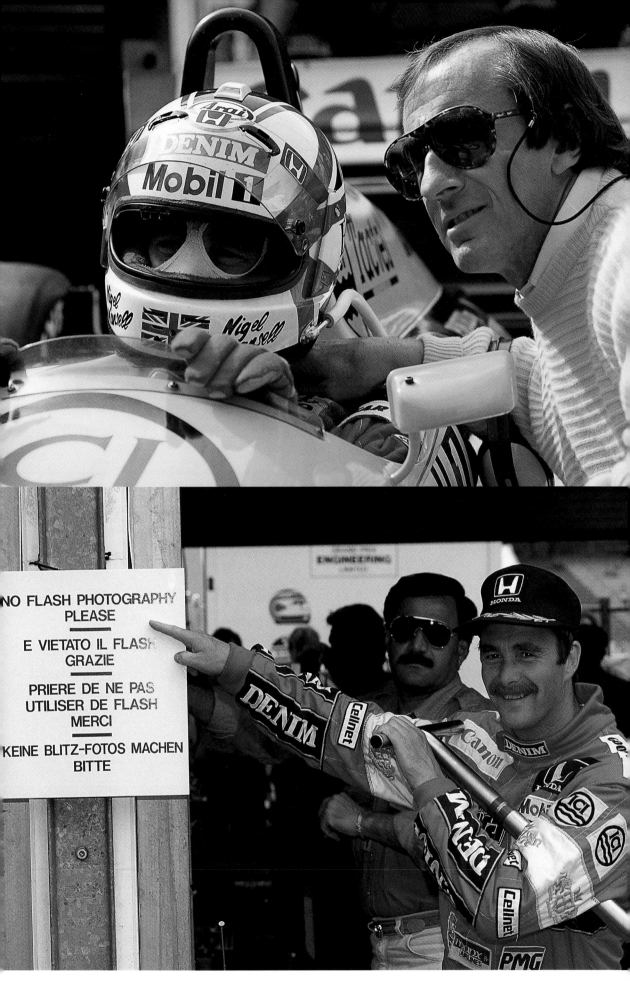

Posing with Jackie Stewart (top) before the 1986 British GP. Still feeling the effects of the concussion from Detroit, Nigel and his medical adviser Dr Rafael Grajales (below) ask photographers not to use flash in the garage

Walking back to the Williams pit to report the drive shaft failure which eliminated him from the 1986 Austrian GP, Nigel offers a little wave to the fans

In Portugal, with three races to go in the 1986 championship, four men (top) were still in with a chance: Senna was soon out of contention, but for Messrs Prost, Mansell and Piquet the fight would go to the last race. BBC's "Voice of F1" Mr Murray Walker (below) tries in vain to be serious during a mass Williams interview in Portugal

Adelaide 1986: the heart-rending moment when tyre failure wiped out Nigel world championship chances when he looked set to win comfortably. An incredulous Alain Prost came through to win the race and the title

Somewhere in the smoke is Nigel, happily "doughnutting" for the fans. Slightly more serious business (below) as he gets his reward for victory at Imola over Senna and Alboreto

Trying to relax in the cramped pit box at Monaco in 1987. Having qualified on pole position, a bad weld on an exhaust pipe forced him to withdraw

Victory from pole position in the French GP of 1987 at Ricard: on the podium with Nigel (below) are Nelson Piquet (who scored the fourth of his seven 2nd places that year) and Alain Prost

They don't necessarily agree with the slogan in Argentina, but who cares, this is Silverstone! On the way (below) to giving the British crowd exactly the result they wanted

Austrian drama: the third (and successful) start, with Piquet narrowly ahead, and (below) striking the titanium skid plates on the bump at the bottom of the hill at the Osterreichring

The start (top) of the Portuguese GP, where Nigel's 1987 fortunes took a dive on lap 14 when his electrics failed. Better luck in Mexico (below), where he defeated Nelson Piquet and Riccardo Patrese to close the gap on his team mate to 12 points

Eliminated from the 1987 Japanese GP by a painful accident during qualifying which forced him to fly home immediately, in Adelaide (below) he was sorely missed by his fans

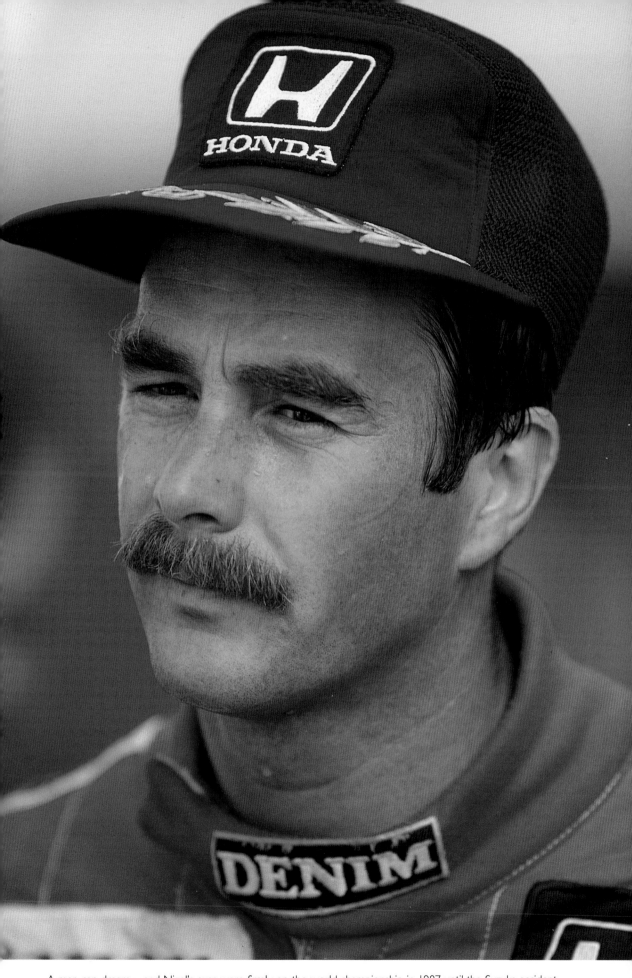

A man can dream – and Nigel's eyes were firmly on the world championship in 1987 until the Suzuka accident.
Due to his injuries, he did not take part in the final race, yet still finished 2nd (to Piquet) in the championship

You can't win 'em all. With only two second places in 1988, including Silverstone (top left), Nigel said goodbye to Williams in Adelaide (centre left). As it happens, it was another second place at Silverstone the following year with Ferrari (bottom left). At Hockenheim in 1988 (top right), an experimental low rear wing was tried in qualifying. Fooling around with fellow-Brit Derek Warwick in '89 and fourth place in the 1990 Brazilian GP (bottom right) after a long pit stop to have a loose anti-roll bar secured

THE MAN THEY CALLED 'IL LEONE' 1988-92

At last, Nigel would become the leading Williams driver. After the two unhappy years with Piquet alongside him, for 1988 he had the comfort of knowing that his Brazilian adversary would be leaving to join Lotus. Unfortunately, also on the move was Honda. The company's completely new turbo V6s would be powering the 'dream team' of Senna and Prost. Deserted by the Japanese, Williams would turn to John Judd and his normally aspirated V8.

Whatever hopes Frank and his men might have had were rapidly dispelled. Having got used to winning, Nigel had to resign himself to losing. The best reason we photographers had for shooting in the Williams pit that year was to catch the 'new' Nigel, who had shaved his moustache. His best results from the 16 races were two second places, one of them a most remarkable achievement in the wet at Silverstone after the suspension of his car had been converted overnight from active to conventional (steel spring) configuration.

A move was called for in 1989, and Ferrari beckoned. Nigel had already been tempted to link up with Maranello once before, in 1986, when he had visited the factory in secret and spoken to Enzo Ferrari himself. Now, although the 'Old Man' was close to the end (he died in August 1988), the Italian public wanted Nigel. The attraction was the exciting new car which had been produced by British designer John Barnard, the genius behind McLaren's past successes. Testing the prototype had started before Nigel even signed, and the car's semi-automatic gearbox was the most advanced of its type.

Unfortunately, his first outings revealed the weakness, even fragility, of the Ferrari V12. Shortly before he departed for the first race, in Brazil, Nigel admitted that the longest run he had been able to do so far had lasted precisely six laps. At the Intercontinental Hotel he quietly approached the British Airways' captain due to command the Sunday evening flight out of Rio and told him to delay takeoff a little. He was so sure the car would break that he intended to be aboard the aircraft.

Of course, the car didn't break and the captain waited in vain. Even Barnard and the Ferrari crew were astonished that the car and engine simply kept on going. By the time the BA flight departed, Nigel was celebrating perhaps his most remarkable victory — on his first outing with Ferrari. It put the seal on what was to be a satisfying season, for although the Ferrari only gave him one more victory – in Hungary – he enjoyed working with Barnard and knowing that their collaboration would pay off in 1990.

For Nigel, one of the enjoyable features of 1989 had been working with Gerhard Berger. He liked the Austrian, even if his unpredictable sense of fun caused a few embarrassments, and he was sad when Gerhard chose to take Alain Prost's place at McLaren in 1990. The 'plus' in this move was that Prost would be coming to Ferrari. Having admired the Frenchman, and considering himself to be his friend, Nigel was genuinely thrilled.

The friendship collapsed almost as soon as Prost had settled in. The Frenchman had already worked with Barnard for two full seasons at McLaren and he did not hesitate to use the experience to take advantage of the Englishman. Unlike Nigel, Prost had a good command of the Italian language, which helped him swiftly to get

Riccardo Patrese gets the treatment from his Canon Williams team mate in Mexico City in March 1992, the second of nine Mansell victories in the season

Second place for the second year running at Monaco in 1992, an irritation, in that it would have been six straight wins were it not for a loose rear wheel – but not much more than an irritation, and some consolation for Senna – in the championship year

comfortable inside the team, with the mechanics and others. It must have been disappointing and hurtful for Nigel to discover that the man he had so respected was, in reality, just as combative towards him as Piquet had been three years earlier. While Prost won five races for Ferrari and remained in contention for the championship right up until his rival Ayrton Senna crashed him off the road at Suzuka, Nigel won only once, in Estoril, Portugal.

After the British GP, having started from pole position and led for 25 laps until his car failed, he called the amazed representatives of the British media to an impromptu press conference in the paddock and announced his retirement. At the age of 37, he said, it was all over. Promising to devote more time to his family, he insisted that Adelaide would be his last race.

With Mansell on the loose, however, Williams immediately showed interest in him. A new partnership with Renault was beginning to pay off for Frank Williams. Nigel's former team was now showing signs of being competitive again. The negotiations started a few days later, with the inevitable result. Forgetting his promises at Silverstone, Nigel allowed his arm to be

twisted. For the appropriate (multi-million) fee, he agreed to rejoin Williams.

Many experts felt that Nigel's move back to Williams represented his last attempt at the championship. When the season started, it looked as though his heart wasn't in it after all. His fans were disappointed when his team mate Riccardo Patrese showed superior form in the first three races of the year. But at Monaco Nigel responded, as he always did, to the challenge of the circuit, finishing second to Senna.

Although he went on to win six races that year, both he and the team slipped up with embarrassing frequency. In Canada he accidentally switched off the ignition while leading, within only a few hundred yards of the finish line. In a tyre-change pit stop in Portugal he was flagged out before a rear wheel had been secured. And in Japan he spun off just when it seemed that he had Senna comfortably beaten.

Nonetheless, the outstanding performance of the Williams-Renault was now clearly established. Having tossed away so many chances in 1991, surely he would not make any mistakes, or at least eliminate enough for outright victory, in the next season?

With five wins in the first five races, Nigel had virtually made sure of the 1992 title before the season had begun. Perhaps his greatest disappointment was Monaco, where a loose rear wheel forced him into the pits with eight laps to go and allowed a grateful Senna to win for the fifth time. Although he still made mistakes, like the desperate lunge at Senna which put him into a sand trap in Canada, this year Nigel could afford them. He secured the championship with a second place in Hungary and would end the season with nine victories.

Nigel was in his 12th season of F1 racing. He had achieved what everybody knew he was capable of doing. But although he was entitled to claim some of the credit for the development that had gone into the Williams FW14B, he was pretty unhappy with any suggestion that he had a superior car, which had gifted him victory. What made him even less happy were the hints that Alain Prost had signed to join the team for 1993. He felt betrayed, especially when Williams attempted to reduce the fee which, he believed, had been negotiated for the next year.

In an emotional outburst at Monza, he declared that he felt badly treated by Frank Williams and Patrick Head and confessed that the relationship between them and him had – irretrievably – broken down. He said he could not make the commitment to Williams required to defend his championship and concluded by saying that he would be considering a change of career, to IndyCars. His final victory of the season, leading all the way in Portugal, lost some of its enjoyment when Prost stole the limelight by revealing that he had signed to take Nigel's place for 1993.

Nigel's announcement soon afterwards that he had agreed terms to drive a Lola-Ford for the Newman-Haas team in the American PPG

Multi-Million Dollar Man. Following a contractual clash with Frank Williams at the end of the '92 season, Mansell walked out of Formula 1 into the arms of Newman-Haas Racing and the PPG IndyCar World Series. It was a huge gamble, but despite his 'rookie' status, Mansell scored five wins and six pole positions in becoming the first driver to secure back-to-back Formula 1 (1992) and IndyCar Championships (1993)

IndyCar championship would disappoint the fans, especially the tens of thousands of flag-waving Britons who had greeted his victory at Silverstone in July by bursting through the crowd control barriers.

But Nigel's mind was made up. It was Goodbye to Europe and Hello to Indy.

Monaco 1988, where Nigel's jinx struck yet again as he was disputing 4th place with Michele Alboreto. In an ambitious passing move, the Italian eliminated the Englishman

The colour and spectacle of F1 racing, (top) on the Jacarepagua circuit in Rio and (below) a Canadian sunset over Montreal and the cold St Laurence river

The Detroit river flows close by the race track during the 1988 Detroit GP as the ill-fated Williams-Judd heads for yet another retirement (this time it was the electrics)

New faces: with first son Leo (top) in 1988, the year that Nigel shaved off the familiar moustache and, in October, resolved to join Ferrari for 1989. Close racing (below) with Senna's more powerful Honda turbo on the way to a fine 2nd place in Spain with the Judd-engined Williams FW12

The Williams crew in action in 1988. There was nothing wrong with the team, but Nigel wanted more power than the Judd V8 could supply. With two 2nd places being his best results, he chose Ferrari for 1989

First time out with Ferrari, in Brazil, Nigel takes on tyres as he heads for the "miraculous" victory with a car that had refused to do more than half a dozen consecutive laps in testing

The debut 1989 win with Ferrari in Brazil cemented the affection for Nigel in Italy, where he became "Il Leone" (the Lion). Nobody could deny that it was a lucky win, assisted by the problems encountered by both of the McLaren-Honda drivers

The banners are out at Imola in 1989, but the Ferrari fans were to be disappointed. Nigel's semi-automatic gear-box failed and Gerhard Berger was hurt in a fiery crash at Tamburello

Phoenix, 1989, and Nigel signals that he's coming into the pits. Once again, the Ferrari's gearbox had failed

Snapshots of 1989, including moments of fun with a Ferrari engineer, the family and a fellow-bobby … and the welcome from the home crowd at Silverstone

Did somebody at the Hungaroring in 1989 know something in advance? Nigel's storming drive (from 12th place on the grid) took even Senna by surprise as he drove his Ferrari brilliantly through the field to win his second GP of the year

The daunting Spa-Francorchamps circuit becomes even more forbidding in the wet. The 1989 Belgian GP found Nigel doing his level best to take on the McLarens of Senna and Prost: he finished 3rd

Two more disappointments from 1989: at Monza (top) before the gearbox failed; and walking back at Estoril (below) after a controversial clash with Ayrton Senna's McLaren

The gloom of the Ferrari garage at Suzuka, where Nigel was running 4th in 1989 when his engine failed

The first of Nigel's two seasons with Ferrari, in 1989, brought him two memorable wins but also too many retirements. It was, he was sure, the basis for a serious championship bid in 1990

Moments from 1990 included leading team mate Alain Prost at Imola (top) and a hard fought 3rd place in Canada behind Senna and Piquet

Having qualified 2nd for the 1990 French GP at Paul Ricard, Nigel dropped out of 5th place with engine trouble

Mobbed at Silverstone by a huge delirious crowd

Hockenheim 1990: meeting the fans (top) before the race, which saw him pulling in to withdraw after a moment across the kerbs which may have damaged the underside of the Ferrari

Heat and frustration in Hungary, where Nigel's 1990 race ended in a clash with the McLaren of Gerhard Berger

Hungarian speed blur (top) and a plea from fans at Spa not to carry through the threat made at Silverstone to give up F1 for good

Ferrari forever: fans show their allegiance at Spa in 1990

Still chasing a victory in 1990, at the Italian GP Nigel had to be content with 4th place. By then the Scuderia's efforts were going into Alain Prost's attempt to win the title from Senna

Estoril 1990 and victory at long last: Nigel shoots the Moet after beating Ayrton Senna fair and square in the Portuguese GP

Lolling in Spain (top): a moment of relaxation shared with Rosanne and Williams press attaché Ann Bradshaw before the 1990 GP at Jerez. Driver's eye view (below) of the Ferrari 641 control console

Cool and heat at Adelaide in 1990. Getting a massage (top) before putting the fire into his courageous drive to 2nd place behind Piquet

After some personal turmoil and heart searching, in November 1990 Nigel accepted Williams' terms and reversed his decision to retire: here he waits to test a Williams-Renault at Estoril in readiness for the 1991 season

Back in a Williams for the first time since 1988, Nigel gets a feel of the Renault-engined FW13B at Estoril in December 1990. He was immediately making changes which dramatically improved the speed of the car

Phoenix, 1991, and Nigel is running 3rd behind Senna and Prost in the US Grand Prix when his gearbox fails

Chasing Senna in a damp Brazilian GP at Interlagos (top), until gearbox problems ended his race.
In pursuit of Senna again (below), this time at Monaco

Rounding the Loews hairpin at Monaco 1991, where he was rewarded with 2nd place behind Senna and his best-ever result in the Principality

Compliments from The Boss at Monaco (top) as Senna greets Nigel after the finish of their 1991 battle. Out in front in Mexico (below), where loss of power cost Nigel a possible win. But with Riccardo Patrese winning it was the first Williams 1-2 for more than two years

Ready for the off at Silverstone in 1991: Nigel's win in the British GP saw him dominate the entire weekend

Silverstone rewards. Nigel gives a ride to Senna (top) after the Brazilian lost 2nd place when his McLaren ran out of fuel on the last lap. A token of appreciation (below) from longtime Williams sponsor Canon

One more than Stirling: Nigel receives the congratulations of Stirling Moss after going one better than the 16 victories scored by the driver who was his lifelong idol

Hockenheim 1991 and Nigel waits to see if anyone will challenge his pole position time. Nobody did and he led (below) virtually all the way to win the German GP from his team mate Patrese

Sprinting back to the pits at Hockenheim after his car stopped in practice, Nigel glances at the track

Double Moet for McLaren chief Ron Dennis from the Williams twins after they took a back seat to Ayrton Senna's come-back victory in the Hungarian GP of 1991

Late summer moments, 1991: sparks in Belgium, where Nigel retired with electrical trouble; meeting Juan Fangio, the sport's only five-times world champion; and back on form at Monza (below, right), where victory over Senna kept him in the championship stakes

A look at the opposition in the mirror at Barcelona in 1991: Nigel's victory in the Spanish GP will certainly count among his greatest

The memorable moment as Nigel goes wheel-to-wheel with Senna down the main straight at Barcelona. The Englishman and his Williams-Renault had the measure of the Brazilian's McLaren-Honda, which was forced to give way as Nigel sped to his fifth and final victory of the 1991 season

Suzuka 1991: Nigel's chances of winning the championship from Senna were already remote, but they vanished altogether as he skated into a gravel trap on lap 10 of the Japanese GP

The Suzuka marshals come to Nigel's assistance after his spin: he was safe but the title was now in the hands of Ayrton Senna

Going for it at Adelaide, Nigel qualified 3rd behind the McLarens at the 1991 Australian GP. When the race was halted in torrential rain after only 14 laps, he was lying 2nd behind Senna

Starting the 1992 season as he meant to continue, Nigel won the South African GP on the rebuilt Kyalami circuit with an all-the-way performance from pole position

Now universally known as "Red Five" (top), Nigel has a pow-wow with friend and longtime associate Peter Windsor, who had his last year as team manager at Williams in 1992

Two more in the book: the Mexican (top) and Brazilian GPs fell to Nigel and his confident handling of the Renault-engined Williams FW14B with its effective electronically-controlled active suspension

Rain in Spain didn't hamper Nigel: while half the field spun off the sodden Barcelona track, his 1992 victory there was his fourth in a row

Watched by Frank Williams (top), Nigel confers with engineer David Brown before venturing (below) out into the rain and the start of his victorious 1992 Spanish GP. Spain was almost always a good venue for Nigel

Wins number 4 and 5 at the start of the 1992 championship season, in Spain (top) and at Imola, where he led all the way for the third time that year

Special delivery in an experimental Renault: Nigel hitches a ride to the pits at Monaco, 1992

Preparing for battle, Monaco 1992

Having led the race to within 7 laps of the finish at Monaco in 1992 (top), Nigel was forced to stop when a rear wheel came loose. In the subsequent chase he exhausted himself trying, but failing, to find a way past race winner Ayrton Senna

Nigel's 1992 Canadian GP came to an undignified end (top) when an attempt to outbrake race leader Senna sent him bouncing over a gravel trap. In discussion (below) with a Renault engineer in Montreal

On the FIA's weigh-in equipment during qualifying for the 1992 French GP at Magny-Cours

Preparing for the race that ended perfectly: Silverstone and the British GP of 1992

This far out in front – on the first lap! Nigel's supremacy in the British GP of 1992 was awe-inspiring. The fans (below) certainly seemed happy about the lack of opposition

On to the track they poured, oblivious (top) to the danger of cars still racing for the line. They loved their True-Brit winner, and he dedicated the race to them

Hockenheim 1992 and win number 8 in the German GP, beating Senna and the Benetton-Ford of Schumacher, seen tucked in behind here (below) soon after one of Nigel's routine pit stops for tyres

Having his feet wiped (top) before he qualifies, Nigel prepares for the Hungarian GP. Second place was more than enough to clinch the title and put smiles on the faces of Renault's engine wizards (below)

Another experimental means of transport was this motorcycle-engined three-wheeler at Monza (top) in 1992. In the garages, the newly crowned champion confers with his crew

Last minute discussion with race engineer David Brown at Estoril before the 1992 Portuguese GP, his ninth and final victory of the season

Monza 1992: the race that got away. After leading the Italian GP for 19 laps, Nigel fell behind team mate Riccardo Patrese and then retired when a hydraulic pump failed. Five laps from the finish the unfortunate Patrese had an identical problem

By the Portuguese GP of 1992, Nigel was barely on speaking terms with the management of the Williams team. But he maintained a deep respect for his engineer, David Brown (top)

Suzuka 1992 and a dominating performance by Williams, who decreed in advance that Riccardo Patrese should win. Having built up a big lead, Nigel duly moved over – only to stop with engine failure. He greets Patrese (below) in the parc fermé

Closer than ever: the final race of the 1992 season found Ayrton Senna's McLaren suddenly competitive again. Nigel had qualified 0.5 second faster, but the two were nose to tail in the race when they collided. Each blamed the other …

The end of the road — or was it? With the championship finally his, Nigel had every intention of walking away from F1 forever in favour of a career in IndyCars

nix, round 2, 1993 (top left). Second oval victory and third of the season at Brooklyn, Michigan in
Is he looking back across the Atlantic? The IndyCar drivers of 1994 (bottom left) European
4 (centre right), an exhausted DNF. The MP4/10 unveiled at the Science Museum in London
e, as always, is right by her husband's sde. Testing at Estoril, March 1995: a distinctly
which did not bode well for the new McLaren challenge

INDY CAR HERO
AND F1 RETURN 1993-95

The arrival of a reigning World Champion on the IndyCar circuit had a magic effect. Having settled his family in Florida, Nigel himself was welcomed everywhere he went. The media interest went sky-high, with foreign journalists and photographers cramming the often modest facilities of the smaller US tracks. When he crashed heavily testing for the first oval race of the 1993 season at Phoenix, the pictures were flashed around the world. The injuries proved to be quite serious, causing him considerable pain in the next few races. His will to recover earned admiration from fellow competitors and fans.

As things turned out, the two years Nigel spent in IndyCar produced starkly different results. Full of enthusiasm in 1993, he won his very first race (Surfers Paradise, in Australia) in front of fans who loved him almost as much as the Silverstone crowd. Back in America and shaking off the effects of the Phoenix accident, he adapted brilliantly to the ovals. The Indianapolis '500' itself was only his second oval

event – yet he was leading when the race entered its final period under the yellow flag. One slip – due his unfamiliarity with re-start procedures – left him standing as Scott Goodyear and Jacques Villeneuve got the jump on him under acceleration. He had to be content with third place.

He scored five wins in 1993, four of them on ovals, defeating Penske drivers Emerson Fittipaldi and Paul Tracy to take the championship. Yet when 1994 started there had been a discernible change in attitude. Part of this was due to the lost competitiveness of the Lola-Ford combination, which could no longer match the Penskes. He fell out with his team mate, the much honoured Mario Andretti, and showed no enthusiasm for testing. Having twice finished in the top three at the beginning of the season, by the end of it he was sometimes scraping in barely in the top six or ten.

Then there was his scary accident at Indianapolis, where another car landed on top of

Under the yellow flag at Long Beach during the 1993 Toyota GP, Nigel Mansell (left) has the inside line on Penske driver Paul Tracy, who went on to score his first IndyCar victory in front of an 85,000-strong crowd. Mansell was not far behind, bringing his Lola-Ford home in 3rd place behind Bobby Rahal

Round 14 of the IndyCar series, Lexington, Ohio, September 1993. Twelfth in the Pioneer Electronics 200 road race. But it was followed by victory at Nazareth a week later, and back-to-back championships. It would be instructive to dig out some of the journalists' sceptical analyses of Mansell's Indy chances written over Christmas '92 …

him during a neutralised period. But most of all there was the lure of Formula 1. With Alain Prost having retired at the end of 1993, GP racing was already short of big names. When Ayrton Senna was killed at Imola, there wasn't a single world champion in the F1 field. The championship needed Nigel, and it was Bernie Ecclestone who helped to make it happen.

Having negotiated a deal with Carl Haas for him to compete in four races with Williams, Nigel arrived in England in the week of the French GP and found himself at Brands Hatch for a test session, preceded by a press conference. The media were there in strength and the crowd that turned out to watch the test was estimated at 5000 – not bad for a Tuesday! His presence at Magny-Cours certainly increased the attendance figures for the French GP.

As far as the Williams team was concerned, Nigel's opinion on the FW16 was vital, even if he never showed signs of being able to outqualify Damon Hill. Sadly, while he drove hard and with commitment, he seemed to have lost the ultimate speed of the old days. Both Hill and Coulthard outshone him at times in those four races. His stamina seemed suspect in the European GP and his memory of the rules was suspect in Japan, where he had a terrific battle with Alesi in the wet only to discover that he

The Old Alliance re-formed, plotting victory in Adelaide, November 1994. Will it be the last time we see Nigel Mansell on the podium – any podium?

had been classified behind the Ferrari because the race had been held in two parts after an accident.

How then did he manage to win at Adelaide? He was in third place, half a minute behind Hill and Schumacher, when their battle for the championship ended in a collision. Nigel came home in first place, being greeted joyfully by fans and old supporters. It had been a lucky result, but it gave him the chance to point out that he wasn't finished yet with Formula 1. There was the lure of a possible second championship.

Because Williams still had an option on his services for 1995 but refused to exercise it, the early part of the winter was an uncomfortable time for Nigel. Finally, he was released by Williams (collecting a worthwhile compensation fee) and in January it was announced that he would race for McLaren.

Within days, Silverstone had sold out of tickets for the British GP. McLaren chief Ron Dennis's ambitious plans for 1995 were based on his new alliance with Mercedes, whose Ilmor V10 engine would power a completely new car. When the MP4/10 was taken to Estoril for its first full test in February, even Nigel's team mate Mika Hakkinen found it a tight fit. For Nigel, though, it was impossible. The seat was too narrow and there wasn't enough elbow room for his energetic driving style. McLaren's crash programme to make a wider monocoque halved

the normal time for such a project (it took just 33 days), but it would not be completed until after the first two races of the season in South America. The wide-body car was ready – just – for Imola. But Nigel was clearly unhappy with the car, and although he managed to struggle to the end of the San Marino GP he had two incidents and was classified two laps behind race winner Damon Hill. He was even less satisfied with the handling of the car at Barcelona for the Spanish GP, to such an extent that he actually pulled into the pits and withdrew. Just over a week later, a statement from McLaren revealed that the contract had been suspended. Nigel and his new team had reached the end of their road together.

At the time of writing, it is impossible to say whether Grand Prix racing will figure in Nigel Mansell's career again. He was ready, he insisted, to accept any suitable offers, and he had not given up hope of racing again at international level. At the same time, he is already busy developing the golf and country club which he has bought at Woodbury in Devon. He is building a new home there for his family, who have settled back into British life.

Whatever the future holds for Nigel Mansell, he has already achieved far more than even he could have imagined, when he and Rosanne took a deep breath and cashed in their savings to buy that first Formula Ford …

The American Way: getting to grips with baseball and making new alliances. When not settling into his Lola-Ford IndyCar, Nigel spent time with team mate Mario Andretti and team owner Paul Newman

Phoenix International Raceway, January 1993, and Nigel gloves up for the first dramatic test on an oval

Surfers Paradise, 1993; in the sun drenched resort of Australia's Gold Coast, Nigel delivered victory on his very first outing in the Newman-Haas Lola-Ford

Celebrating at Surfers with Emerson Fittipaldi (top left) and Robby Gordon. Back in the USA (below) with the Lola at Phoenix

A test-session accident at Phoenix in April sent Nigel crashing into the wall. The flames were sparked when hot oil showered from the shattered gearbox

The hole in the Phoenix wall (top), which yielded to an impact at more than 150 mph. Nigel is stretchered away with injuries that would bother him for months

With five wins in his first year at Indy, Nigel could be pleased. At Portland, nevertheless, he needed a bit of encouragement (below left) from Ford chief Michael Kranefuss

Pit work (top) at New Hampshire, where Nigel had a nerve-tingling win on the tiny oval, proving once and for all that he could handle US-style racing. He was equally adept on road circuits like Elkhart Lake (below), although he had to give best this time to the Penske of Paul Tracy

Lexington, Ohio, in September 1993. Nigel pushing hard to make up for time lost in a first lap collision with Paul Tracy's Penske

Another bullring, this time at Nazareth, Pennsylvania in September 1993. Nigel again mastered the intricacies of oval racing to take the glassware (below) from Canadians Scott Goodyear and Paul Tracy

Celebrating with Carl Haas and the crew (top) after the Nazareth race. More serious discussions, this time at Monterey (below), with his race engineer

October 1993 saw Nigel's first British racing appearance of the season, as a guest driver with one of Andy Rouse's BTCC Ford Mondeos at Donington Park. The fans showed their appreciation by packing the circuit

The race didn't go as well as might have been expected. After an "off" in qualifying (above), he crashed heavily in the race and was briefly unconscious

The 1994 IndyCar season found Nigel in a less enthusiastic mood. The Lola-Ford was less competitive than in 1993 and after a 3rd place behind the Penske men Fittipaldi and Unser at Phoenix (centre left), Nigel seemed, from a distance at least, to lose interest

One of Nigel's two 2nd places in 1994 was scored at Cleveland, where the Lola was a little more competitive but still not on the pace with race winner Al Unser's Penske-Ilmor

The 1994 New England Slick 50 at New Hampshire (top) and the Molson Indy in Vancouver (below) both saw DNFs for Nigel, whose second season of Indy racing ended with a depressing 8th place in the PPG Cup

Putting a brave face on it before the final IndyCar race of the season at Monterey in California (top), Nigel and team-mate Mario Andretti force a smile. In the race he was classified 8th

In four "guest" races with Williams and Renault in 1994, Nigel had the opportunity to meet former Ferrari team mate Alain Prost (top) – and he was soon in the thick of the action. All the bravado was back with a hard-fought 4th place in the wet at Suzuka (below left) and – at Adelaide (below right) – a magical, though to be objective, unexpected, victory

A champagne shower for Nigel at Adelaide, courtesy of Gerhard Berger (2nd) and Martin Brundle (right)

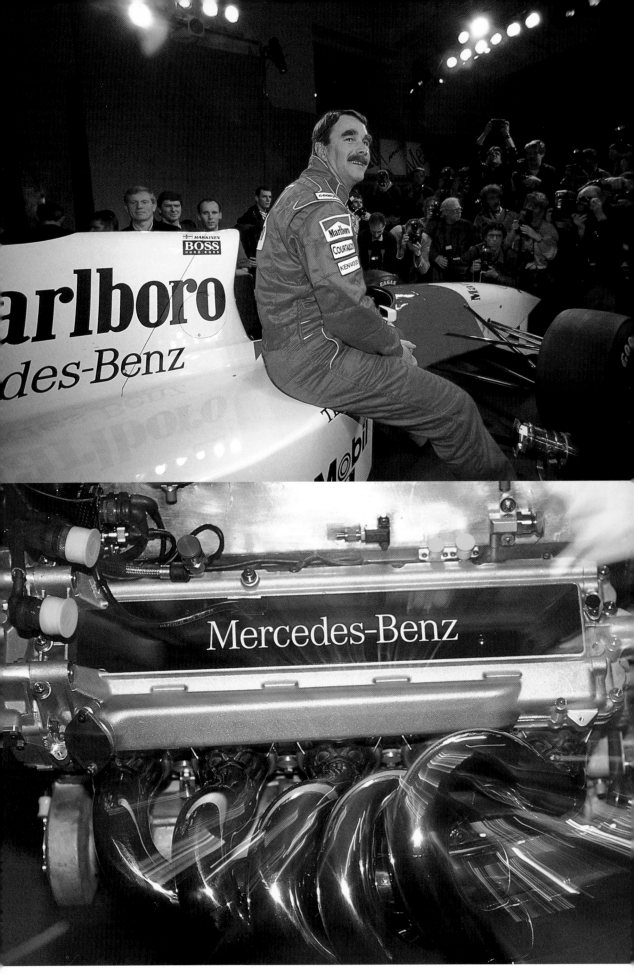

London's Science Museum was the venue for the unveiling of the unconventional McLaren MP4/10 and its all-new V10 Mercedes engine. "If it goes half as quick as it looks, everyone had better watch out," said Nigel

Nigel's first test with the MP4/10 at Estoril revealed the uncomfortable truth that the MP4/10 was not only uncompetitive but its monocoque was too narrow to accommodate the driver. Nigel's F1 debut with McLaren had to be postponed for two races

One minute's silence on the grid at Imola on April 30, 1995 (top), to remember those who had died there one year earlier. A new partner, Mika Hakkinen (below), who also found the cockpit very cramped. Nigel was still unhappy with the handling and retired after an incident with Jordan-Peugeot driver Eddie Irvine

After telling McLaren chief Ron Dennis (top) what was wrong with the MP4/10, the international media (below) demanded to hear the same story from Nigel for public consumption

In a press conference at Barcelona (top), Nigel had to check with Ron Dennis before he made certain cautious remarks about the imperfections in the revised MP4/10. In the race (below) he pulled out after a straight-on moment and had to admit that he didn't trust the car's handling

Watching the progress of his rivals in the McLaren garage at Barcelona. A week later, he and McLaren announced that they had decided to part "by mutual consent." Will we see him back? Only time will tell …

NIGEL MANSELL CAREER RECORD

1976

ENTRANT: Nigel Mansell
CAR: Hawke DL11-Ford (FF1600)

Pos	Race	Date	Circuit
1	FF1600 Reserve's Race	29.05.76	Mallory Park
1	Dunlop Star of Tomorrow *Ht 1*	10.07.76	Castle Combe
6	Dunlop Star of Tomorrow *Final*	10.07.76	Castle Combe
1	Dalsun Limited FF1600 Race	12.08.76	Castle Combe
1	Dunlop Star of Tomorrow *Ht 2*	17.08.76	Oulton Park
1	Dunlop Star of Tomorrow *Final*	17.08.76	Oulton Park
2	FF1600 Race	19.08.76	Mallory Park

1977

ENTRANT: Patrick Mulleady
CAR: Javelin JL5-Ford (FF1600)

Pos	Race	Date	Circuit
dns	Brush Fusegear FF1600	06.03.77	Silverstone
3	Townsend-Thoresen *Ht 1*	13.03.77	Oulton Park
3	Townsend-Thoresen *Final*	13.03.77	Oulton Park
2	Brush Fusegear FF1600 *Ht 1*	20.03.77	Silverstone
2	Brush Fusegear FF1600 *Final*	20.03.77	Silverstone
3	Townsend-Thoresen *Ht 2*	27.03.77	Snetterton
ret	Townsend-Thoresen *Final*	27.03.77	Snetterton
5	BARC FF1600	03.04.77	Silverstone
4	Townsend-Thoresen FF1600	10.04.77	Snetterton
2	BARC FF1600	11.04.77	Thruxton
1	Brush Fusegear FF1600 *Ht 1*	01.05.77	Brands Hatch
3	Brush Fusegear FF1600 *Final*	01.05.77	Brands Hatch
ret	Townsend-Thoresen *Ht 2*	07.05.77	Oulton Park

ENTRANT: Alan McKechnie
CAR: Crossle 32F-Ford (FF1600)
   except as indicated •Crossle 25F-Ford

Pos	Race	Date	Circuit
1	Brush Fusegear FF1600•	08.05.77	Thruxton
nc	Brush Fusegear FF1600 *Ht 2*•	15.05.77	Silverstone
1	Brush Fusegear FF1600 *Ht 1*•	22.05.77	Oulton Park
ret	Brush Fusegear FF1600 *Final*•	22.05.77	Oulton Park
1	Townsend-Thoresen *Ht 1*•	23.05.77	Brands Hatch
ret	Townsend-Thoresen *Final*•	23.05.77	Brands Hatch
2	Townsend-Thoresen *Ht 2*	24.07.77	Brands Hatch
4	Townsend-Thoresen *Final*	24.07.77	Brands Hatch
1	BARC FF1600 *Ht 3*	31.07.77	Donington Park
1	BARC FF1600 *Final*	31.07.77	Donington Park
2	Brush Fusegear FF1600 *Ht 1*	07.08.77	Donington Park
1	Brush Fusegear FF1600 *Final*	07.08.77	Donington Park
3	Townsend-Thoresen *Ht 1*	20.08.77	Oulton Park
2	Townsend-Thoresen *Final*	20.08.77	Oulton Park
1	Brush Fusegear FF1600 *Ht 3*	21.08.77	Mallory Park
1	Brush Fusegear FF1600 *Final*	21.08.77	Mallory Park
ret	European/Vandervell F3 *Ht 1* (Car: Puma 377-Toyota)	27.08.77	Donington Park
1	Brush Fusegear FF1600 *Ht 3*	27.08.77	Donington Park
2	Brush Fusegear FF1600 *Final*	27.08.77	Donington Park
ret	Vandervell F3 (Car: Puma 377-Toyota)	29.08.77	Silverstone
1	Brush Fusegear FF1600 *Ht 2*	29.08.77	Silverstone
2	Brush Fusegear FF1600 *Final*	29.08.77	Silverstone
1	Townsend-Thoresen *Ht 1*	04.09.77	Mallory Park
1	Townsend-Thoresen *Final*	04.09.77	Mallory Park
2	Brush Fusegear FF1600 *Ht 2*	11.09.77	Donington Park
1	Brush Fusegear FF1600 *Final*	11.09.77	Donington Park
1	BARC FF1600 *Ht 2*	24.09.77	Oulton Park
1	BARC FF1600 *Final*	24.09.77	Oulton Park
4	Vandervell F3 (Car: Lola T570-Toyota)	01.10.77	Silverstone
1	Brush Fusegear FF1600	01.10.77	Silverstone
1	Non-Championship FF1600 Race	02.10.77	Donington Park
10	BP F3 (Car: Lola T570-Toyota)	30.10.77	Thruxton
1	BARC FF1600	30.10.77	Thruxton
ret	FF1600 Festival *Ht 1*	06.11.77	Brands Hatch
5	Non-Championship F3 Race (Car: Lola T570-Toyota)	13.11.77	Thruxton
1	Non-Championship FF1600 Race	13.11.77	Thruxton

1978

ENTRANT: March Engineering (except 25.06.78)
CAR: March 783-Toyota

Pos	Race	Date	Circuit
2	Vandervell F3	19.03.78	Silverstone
7	BP F3	27.03.78	Thruxton
7	BP F3	16.04.78	Brands Hatch
7	BP F3	22.04.78	Oulton Park
4	BP F3	30.04.78	Donington Park
dnq	Donington '£50,000' F2 Race (Car: Chevron B42-Hart)	25.06.78	Donington Park

1979

ENTRANT: Unipart Racing Team
CAR: March 783/793-Triumph

Pos	Race	Date	Circuit
11	Vandervell F3	04.03.79	Silverstone
2	Vandervell F3	11.03.79	Thruxton
1	Vandervell F3	25.03.79	Silverstone
8	Vandervell F3	01.04.79	Snetterton
7	Vandervell F3	08.04.79	Donington Park
4	Vandervell F3	16.04.79	Thruxton
6	Vandervell F3	07.05.79	Brands Hatch
6	European/Vandervell F3 Ht 1	20.05.79	Donington Park
ret	European/Vandervell F3 Final	20.05.79	Donington Park
11	Monaco F3	26.05.79	Monte Carlo
4	Vandervell F3	10.06.79	Brands Hatch
ret	Vandervell F3	17.06.79	Cadwell Park
8	Vandervell F3	01.07.79	Silverstone
6	Vandervell F3	14.07.79	Silverstone
6	Vandervell F3	27.08.79	Silverstone
2	Non-Championship F3 Race	09.09.79	Donington Park
ret	Vandervell F3	15.09.79	Oulton Park
8	Vandervell F3	28.10.79	Thruxton
ret	STP Products F3	03.11.79	Thruxton

1980

ENTRANT: March Engineering
CAR: March 803-Toyota

Pos	Race	Date	Circuit
4	Vandervell F3	02.03.80	Silverstone
4	Vandervell F3	09.03.80	Thruxton
4	Vandervell F3	30.03.80	Brands Hatch
5	Vandervell F3	07.04.80	Thruxton
6	Vandervell F3	20.04.80	Silverstone
ret	Vandervell F3	06.05.80	Thruxton
6	Vandervell F3	11.05.80	Snetterton
8	Monaco F3	17.05.80	Monte Carlo
6	Vandervell F3	26.05.80	Silverstone

ENTRANT: Ralt Cars Limited
CAR: Ralt RH6-Honda

Pos	Race	Date	Circuit
11	Marlboro F2 Trophy	08.06.80	Silverstone
ret	Grote Prijs van Limborg F2	22.06.80	Zolder
5	Grote Prijs van Zandvoort F2	20.07.80	Zandvoort
2	Preis von Baden-Wurttenburg F2	28.09.80	Hockenheim

ENTRANT: Team Essex Lotus
CAR: Lotus 81/81B-Cosworth DFV

Pos	Race	Date	Circuit
ret	Austrian GP	17.08.80	Osterreichring
ret	Dutch GP	31.08.80	Zandvoort
dnq	Italian GP	13.09.80	Imola

1981

ENTRANT: Team Essex Lotus/John Player Team Lotus
CAR: •Lotus 81-Cosworth DFV
     Lotus 87-Cosworth DFV

Pos	Race	Date	Circuit
10	South African GP•	07.03.81	Kyalami
ret	US GP West•	15.03.81	Long Beach
11	Brazilian GP•	29.03.81	Rio
ret	Argentine GP•	12.04.81	Buenos Aires
3	Belgian GP•	17.05.81	Zolder
ret	Monaco GP	31.05.81	Monte Carlo
6	Spanish GP (now JP Team Lotus)	21.06.81	Jarama
7	French GP	05.07.81	Dijon
dnq	British GP	18.07.81	Silverstone
dsq	British GP	18.07.81	Silverstone
	(Lotus 88B; dsq during practice)		
ret	German GP	02.08.81	Hockenheim
ret	Austrian GP	16.08.81	Osterreichring
ret	Dutch GP	30.08.81	Zandvoort
ret	Italian GP	13.09.81	Monza
ret	Canadian GP	27.09.81	Montreal
4	Caesar's Palace GP	17.10.81	Las Vegas

1982

ENTRANT: John Player Team Lotus
CAR: Lotus 91-Cosworth DFV

Pos	Race	Date	Circuit
ret	South African GP (Lotus 87B)	23.01.82	Kyalami
3	Brazilian GP	21.03.82	Rio
7	US GP West	04.04.82	Long Beach
3*	Belgian GP	09.05.82	Zolder
4	Monaco GP	23.05.82	Monte Carlo
ret	US GP (Detroit)	06.06.82	Detroit
ret	Canadian GP	13.06.82	Montreal
ret	British GP	18.07.82	Brands Hatch
9	German GP	08.08.82	Hockenheim
ret	Austrian GP	15.08.82	Osterreichring
8	Swiss GP	29.08.82	Dijon
7	Italian GP	12.09.82	Monza
ret	Caesar's Palace GP	25.09.82	Las Vegas

KEY   * retired   dnf did not finish   dnq did not qualify   dsq disqualified   dns did not start   nc not classified   ret retired   susp suspended

1983

Entrant: John Player Team Lotus
Car: *Lotus 92-Cosworth DFV
Lotus 94T-Renault EFI unless otherwise indicated

Pos	Race	Date	Circuit
12	Brazilian GP*	13.03.83	Rio
12	US GP West*	27.03.83	Long Beach
ret	Race of Champions*	10.04.83	Brands Hatch
ret	French GP*	17.04.83	Paul Ricard
ret	San Marino GP*	01.05.83	Imola
ret	Monaco GP*	15.05.83	Monte Carlo
ret	Belgian GP*	22.05.83	Spa
6	US GP (Detroit)*	05.06.83	Detroit
ret	Canadian GP*	12.06.83	Montreal
4	British GP	16.07.83	Silverstone
ret	German GP	07.08.83	Hockenheim
dns	German GP (Lotus 93T-Renault EFI, practice only)		
5	Austrian GP	14.08.83	Osterreichring
ret	Dutch GP	28.08.83	Zandvoort
8	Italian GP	11.09.83	Monza
3	European GP	25.09.83	Brands Hatch
nc	South African GP	15.10.83	Kyalami

1984

Entrant: John Player Team Lotus
Car: Lotus 95T-Renault EF4

Pos	Race	Date	Circuit
ret	Brazilian GP	25.03.84	Rio
ret	SouthAfrican GP	07.04.84	Kyalami
ret	Belgian GP	29.04.84	Zolder
ret	SanMarino GP	06.05.84	Imola
3	French GP	20.05.84	Dijon
ret	Monaco GP	03.06.84	Monte Carlo
6	Canadian GP	17.06.84	Montreal
ret	US GP (Detroit)	24.06.84	Detroit
6*	US GP (Dallas)	08.07.84	Dallas
ret	British GP	22.07.84	Brands Hatch
4	German GP	05.08.84	Hockenheim
ret	Austrian GP	19.08.84	Osterreichring
3	Dutch GP	26.08.84	Zandvoort
ret	Italian GP	09.09.84	Monza
ret	European GP	07.10.84	Nurburgring
ret	Portuguese GP	21.10.84	Estoril

What are they all straining to catch a glimpse of? It's Dallas, 1984, and Nigel Mansell has collapsed on the track after a forlorn attempt to push his Lotus to the finish line in the searing heat. A wasted effort you could say, in that it's against the rules. Go ahead and say it: if you can't see that commitment for what it is …

1985

ENTRANT: Canon Williams Honda Team
CAR: Williams FW10-Honda RA 163-3

Pos	Race	Date	Circuit
ret	Brazilian GP	07.04.85	Rio
5	Portuguese GP	21.04.85	Estoril
5	San Marino GP	05.05.85	Imola
7	Monaco GP	19.05.85	Monte Carlo
6	Canadian GP	16.06.85	Montreal
ret	US GP (Detroit)	23.06.85	Detroit
dns	French GP	07.07.85	Paul Ricard
ret	British GP	21.07.85	Silverstone
6	German GP	04.08.85	Nurburgring
ret	Austrian GP	18.08.85	Osterreichring
6	Dutch GP	25.08.85	Zandvoort
11*	Italian GP	08.09.85	Monza
2	Belgian GP	15.09.85	Spa
1	European GP	06.10.85	Brands Hatch
1	South African GP	19.10.85	Kyalami
ret	Australian GP	03.11.85	Adelaide

1987

ENTRANT: Canon Williams Honda Team
CAR: Williams FW11B-Honda RA 166-G

Pos	Race	Date	Circuit
6	Brazilian GP (Honda RA 166-E)	12.04.87	Rio
1	San Marino GP	03.05.87	Imola
ret	Belgian GP	17.05.87	Spa
ret	Monaco GP	31.05.87	Monte Carlo
5	US GP (Detroit)	21.06.87	Detroit
1	French GP	05.07.87	Paul Ricard
1	British GP	12.07.87	Silverstone
ret	German GP	26.07.87	Hockenheim
14*	Hungarian GP	09.08.87	Hungaroring
1	Austrian GP	16.08.87	Osterreichring
3	Italian GP	06.09.87	Monza
ret	Portuguese GP	20.09.87	Estoril
1	Spanish GP	27.09.87	Jerez
1	Mexican GP	18.10.87	Mexico City
dns	Japanese GP	01.11.87	Suzuka
dns	Australian GP	15.11.87	Adelaide

1986

ENTRANT: Canon Williams Honda Team
CAR: Williams FW11-Honda RA 166-E

Pos	Race	Date	Circuit
ret	Brazilian GP	23.03.86	Rio
2	Spanish GP	13.04.86	Jerez
ret	San Marino GP	27.04.86	Imola
4	Monaco GP	11.05.86	Monte Carlo
1	Belgian GP	25.05.86	Spa
1	Canadian GP	15.06.86	Montreal
5	US GP (Detroit)	22.06.86	Detroit
1	French GP	06.07.86	Paul Ricard
1	British GP	13.07.86	Brands Hatch
3	German GP	27.07.86	Hockenheim
3	Hungarian GP	10.08.86	Hungaroring
ret	Austrian GP	17.08.86	Osterreichring
2	Italian GP	07.09.86	Monza
1	Portuguese GP	21.09.86	Estoril
5	Mexican GP	12.10.86	Mexico City
ret	Australian GP	26.10.86	Adelaide

1988

ENTRANT: Canon Williams Honda Team
CAR: Williams FW12-Judd CV

Pos	Race	Date	Circuit
ret	Brazilian GP	03.04.88	Rio
ret	San Marino GP	01.05.88	Imola
ret	Monaco GP	15.05.88	Monte Carlo
ret	Mexican GP	29.05.88	Mexico City
ret	Canadian GP	12.06.88	Montreal
ret	US GP (Detroit)	19.06.88	Detroit
ret	French GP	03.07.88	Paul Ricard
2	British GP	10.07.88	Silverstone
ret	German GP	24.07.88	Hockenheim
ret	Hungarian GP	07.08.88	Hungaroring
ret	Belgian GP	28.08.88	Spa
ret	Italian GP	11.09.88	Monza
ret	Portuguese GP	25.09.88	Estoril
2	Spanish GP	02.10.88	Jerez
ret	Japanese GP	30.10.88	Suzuka
ret	Australian GP	13.11.88	Adelaide

KEY   * retired   **dnf** did not finish   **dnq** did not qualify   **dsq** disqualified   **dns** did not start   **nc** not classified   **ret** retired   **susp** suspended

1989

ENTRANT: Ferrari, Fiat, Agip, Marlboro
CAR: Ferrari 640-Ferrari V12 Tipo 034

Pos	Race	Date	Circuit
I	Brazilian GP	26.03.89	Rio
ret	San Marino GP	23.04.89	Imola
ret	Monaco GP	07.05.89	Monte Carlo
ret	Mexican GP	28.05.89	Mexico City
ret	US GP (Phoenix)	04.06.89	Phoenix
dsq	Canadian GP	18.06.89	Montreal
2	French GP	09.07.89	Paul Ricard
2	British GP	16.07.89	Silverstone
3	German GP	30.07.89	Hockenheim
I	Hungarian GP	13.08.89	Hangaroring
3	Belgian GP	27.08.89	Spa
ret	Italian GP	10.09.89	Monza
dsq	Portuguese GP	24.09.89	Estoril
susp	Spanish GP	01.10.89	Jerez
ret	Japanese GP	22.10.89	Suzuka
ret	Australian GP	05.11.89	Adelaide

1991

ENTRANT: Canon Williams Team
CAR: Williams-Renault FW14

Pos	Race	Date	Circuit
ret	US GP	10.03.91	Phoenix
ret	Brazilian GP	24.03.91	Interlagos
ret	San Marino GP	28.04.91	Imola
2	Monaco GP	12.05.91	Monte Carlo
6	Canadian GP	02.06.91	Montreal
2	Mexican GP	16.06.91	Mexico City
I	French GP	07.07.91	Magny-Cours
I	British GP	14.07.91	Silverstone
I	German GP	28.07.91	Hockenheim
2	Hungarian GP	11.08.91	Hungaroring
ret	Belgian GP	25.08.91	Spa
I	Italian GP	08.09.91	Monza
dsq	Portuguese GP	22.09.91	Estoril
I	Spanish GP	10.10.91	Barcelona
ret	Japanese GP	21.10.91	Suzuka
2	Australian GP	03.11.91	Adelaide

1990

ENTRANT: Ferrari, Fiat, Agip, Marlboro
CAR: Ferrari 641-Ferrari V12 Tipo 037

Pos	Race	Date	Circuit
ret	US GP (Phoenix)	11.03.90	Phoenix
4	Brazilian GP	25.03.90	Interlagos
ret	San Marino GP	13.05.90	Imola
ret	Monaco GP	27.05.90	Monte Carlo
3	Canadian GP	10.06.90	Montreal
2	Mexican GP	24.06.90	Mexico City
ret	French GP	08.07.90	Paul Ricard
ret	British GP	15.07.90	Silverstone
ret	German GP	29.07.90	Hockenheim
ret	Hungarian GP	12.08.90	Hungaroring
ret	Belgian GP	26.08.90	Spa
4	Italian GP	09.09.90	Monza
I	Portuguese GP	23.09.90	Estoril
2	Spanish GP	30.09.90	Jerez
ret	Japanese GP	21.10.90	Suzuka
2	Australian GP	04.11.90	Adelaide

1992

ENTRANT: Canon Williams Team
CAR: Williams-Renault FW14B

Pos	Race	Date	Circuit
I	South African GP	01.03.92	Kyalami
I	Mexican GP	22.03.92	Mexico City
I	Brazilian GP	05.04.92	Brazil
I	Spanish GP	03.05.92	Barcelona
I	San Marino GP	17.05.92	Imola
2	Monaco GP	31.05.92	Monte Carlo
dnf	Canadian GP	14.06.92	Montreal
I	French GP	05.07.92	Magny-Cours
I	British GP	12.07.92	Silverstone
I	German GP	26.07.92	Hockenheim
2	Hungarian GP	16.08.92	Hungaroring
2	Belgian GP	30.08.92	Spa-F'champs
dnf	Italian GP	13.09.92	Monza
I	Portuguese GP	27.09.92	Estoril
ret	Japanese GP	25.10.92	Suzuka
ret	Australian GP	08.11.92	Adelaide

1993

PPG Indy Car World Series Championship
ENTRANT: Newman-Hass Racing, K-mart, Havoline
CAR: Lola Ford Cosworth T93/00 XB

Pos	Race	Date	Circuit
1	Australian FIA Indy Car GP (road)	21.03.93	Surfers Paradise
wdn	Valvoline 200 (oval)	04.04.93	Phoenix, AZ
3	Toyota GP (road)	18.04.93	Long Beach, CA
3	Indianapolis 500 (oval)	30.05.93	Indianapolis, IN
1	Miller Genuine Draft 200 (oval)	06.06.93	Milwaukee, WI
15*	ITT Automotive Detroit GP (road)	13.06.93	Detroit, MI
2	Budweiser/G.I. Joe's 200 (road)	27.06.93	Portland, OR
3	Budweiser GP of Cleveland (road)	11.07.93	Cleveland, OH
20*	Molson Indy Toronto (road)	18.07.93	Toronto, Canada
1	Marlboro 500 (oval)	01.08.93	Brooklyn, MI
1	New England 200 (oval)	08.08.93	Loudon, NH
2	Texaco/Havoline 200 (road)	22.08.93	Elkhart Lake, WI
6	Molson Indy Vancouver (road)	29.08.93	Vancouver, Canada
12	Pioneer Electronics 200 (road)	12.09.93	Lexington, OH
1	Bosch Spark Plug GP (oval)	19.09.93	Nazareth, PA
23*	Makita/Toyota Monterey GP (road)	03.10.93	Monterey, CA

ENTRANT: Team Mondeo/Ford Electronics and ICS
CAR: Ford Mondeo Ghia

Pos	Race	Date	Circuit
ret	RAC BTCC TOCA Shootout	16.10.93	Donington Park

1994

ENTRANT: Newman-Hass Racing, K-mart, Havoline
CAR: Lola Ford Cosworth T94/00 XB

Pos	Race	Date	Circuit
9	Australian FIA Indy Car GP (road)	20.03.94	Surfers' Paradise
3	Slick-50 200 (oval)	10.04.94	Phoenix, AZ
2	Toyota GP (road)	17.04.94	Long Beach, CA
22*	Indianapolis 500 (oval)	29.05.94	Indianapolis, IN
5	Miller Genuine Draft 200 (oval)	05.06.94	Milwaukee, WI
21*	ITT Automotive Detroit GP (road)	12.06.94	Detroit, MI
5	Budweiser/G.I. Joe's 200 (road)	26.07.94	Portland, OR
2	Budweiser GP of Cleveland (road)	10.07.94	Cleveland, OH
23*	Molson Indy Toronto (road)	17.07.94	Toronto, Canada
26*	Marlboro 500 (oval)	31.07.94	Brooklyn, MI
7	Miller Genuine Draft 200 (Road)	14.08.94	Lexington, OH
18*	Slick-50 200 (oval)	21.08.94	Loudon, NH
10*	Molson Indy Vancouver (road)	04.09.94	Vancouver, Canada
13	Texaco/Havoline 200 (road)	11.09.94	ElkhartLake, WI
22*	Bosch Spark Plug GP (oval)	18.09.94	Nazareth, PA
8	Toyota Monterey GP (road)	09.10.94	Monterey, CA

ENTRANT: Rothmans Williams Renault
CAR: Williams FW16B-Renault RS6C V10

Pos	Race	Date	Circuit
ret	French GP (FW16 RS6 V10)	03.07.94	Magny-Cours
ret	European GP	16.10.94	Jerez
4	Japanese GP	06.11.94	Suzuka
1	Australian GP	13.11.94	Adelaide

1995

ENTRANT: McLaren-Mercedes
CAR: MP4/10-V1

Pos	Race	Date	Circuit
10	San Marino GP	30.04.95	Imola
ret	Spanish GP	14.05.95	Barcelona

Championship records

Formula1 World Championship placings
1st-6th + pole + fastest lap

Races	187
1st	31
2nd	17
3rd	11
4th	8
5th	6
6th	9
pole	32
Fastest lap	30
Failed to qualify	2

Formula 1 positions

1981	14th
1982	14th
1983	12th
1984	9th
1985	6th
1986	2nd
1987	2nd
1988	9th
1989	4th
1990	5th
1991	2nd
1992	1st
1994	9th

Indy Car positions

1993	1st
1994	8th

KEY   * retired   dnf did not finish   dnq did not qualify   dsq disqualified   dns did not start   nc not classified   ret retired   susp suspended

1982

1983

1984

1985

1986

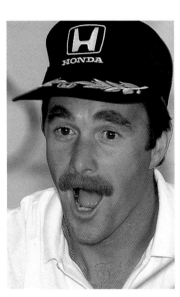

1987

1988

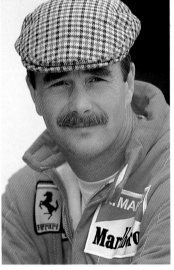

1989

1990

1991

1992

1993

1994

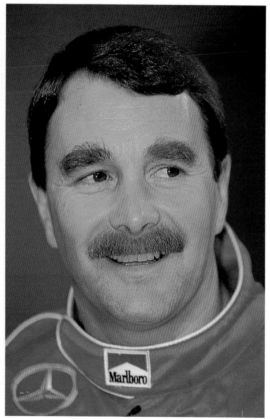

1995

No, not the salute of triumph in this case. DNF at Montreal in 1992. But behind the closed eyes, the knowledge that the prize was finally within his grasp. What a journey it had been to that moment – and what drama was yet to come